# Called to Courage

D1608853

PROJECT SPONSORS

Missouri Center for the Book

Western Historical Manuscript Collection,
University of Missouri–Columbia


SPECIAL THANKS

Dan Glover, Graphic Artist, College of Arts and Science,
University of Missouri–Columbia

Father Phil Hoebing,
Quincy University

Howard W. Marshall, Professor Emeritus,
University of Missouri–Columbia

Chris Montgomery, Photographic Specialist,
State Historical Society of Missouri, Columbia

Claudia Powell, Graphic Specialist,
Western Historical Manuscript Collection–Columbia

Adolf E. Schroeder, Professor Emeritus,
University of Missouri–Columbia

## MISSOURI HERITAGE READERS
### General Editor, Rebecca B. Schroeder

Each Missouri Heritage Reader explores a particular aspect of the state's rich cultural heritage. Focusing on people, places, historical events, and the details of daily life, these books illustrate the ways in which people from all parts of the world contributed to the development of the state and the region. The books incorporate documentary and oral history, folklore, and informal literature in a way that makes these resources accessible to all Missourians.

Intended primarily for adult new readers, these books will also be invaluable to readers of all ages interested in the cultural and social history of Missouri.

# BOOKS IN THE SERIES

# Called to Courage

Four Women in Missouri History

Margot Ford McMillen and
Heather Roberson

University of Missouri Press
Columbia and London

Library of Congress Cataloging-in-Publication Data

McMillen, Margot Ford.
Called to courage : four women in Missouri history
/ Margot Ford McMillen and Heather Roberson.
p.   cm.—(Missouri heritage readers)
Includes index.
Contents: Ignon Ouaconisen, or, Françoise of the Missouri Nation—Olive
Vanbibber Boone—Martha Jane Chisley Tolton—Nell Donnelly Reed.
ISBN 0-8262-1399-5 (alk. paper)
1. Women pioneers—Missouri—Biography.   2. Ignon Ouaconisen, ca.
1700–ca. 1751.   3. Boone, Olive Van Bibber, 1783–1858.   4. Tolton,
Martha Jane Chisley, b. 1833.   5. Reed, Nell Donnelly, b. 1889.   6.
Missouri—Biography.   I. Roberson, Heather.   II. Title.   III. Series.
CT3260 .M36 2002
920.72'09778—dc21
[B]                                                                      2002017952

Designer: Kristie Lee
Typesetter: BOOKCOMP, Inc.
Printer and binder: Thomson-Shore, Inc.
Typefaces: Adobe Garamond, Poppl-Exquisit Regular

*To all those called to courage,*
*Their stories told*
*Or forgotten.*

# Contents

# Acknowledgments

The four women featured in this book blazed trails, persevered through the toughest circumstances, and left stories that changed history, and we are grateful to the many people who have helped us understand their lives and times. We received help from many generous researchers, some of whom had written about history from the masculine point of view and were now challenged to think about "the rest of the story."

We especially thank the Frank Norall family, who answered Margot's questions about Ignon Ouaconisen. Thank you to John Mack Faragher for his generous advice to Heather while she explored the life of Olive Boone, and to Rachel Penn at the Nathan Boone State Historical Site. Our thanks to Fae Sotham and Chris Montgomery of the State Historical Society of Missouri in Columbia, and to David Moore, Bill Stolz, and Peter McCarthy of the Western Historical Manuscript Collection at the University of Missouri–Columbia and to David Boutros at the University of Missouri–Kansas City. Thank you also to Patricia Tomczak, Quincy University Archives, Brenner Library, and to Professor Emeritus Howard Marshall of UMC, always our first reader.

We would also like to thank Rebecca Schroeder, general editor of the Missouri Heritage Readers series, and we appreciate the contributions of Julie Schroeder of the University of Missouri Press, which publishes this series celebrating the diversity of Missouri history.

*Called to Courage*

# *Introduction*

The four women in this book have forged trails for the rest of us. From their times to ours, those trails have become paved roads and superhighways to a wide variety of goals. Today, women are running farms and construction firms, producing movies, and writing books. As many women as men are earning degrees in medicine, law, and other professions. At the same time, men are free to pursue nontraditional careers or even stay home and raise kids as house fathers. Everyone benefits from the new opportunities the women in this book helped to create.

We have come to understand that the women in this book were exceptional because they had the courage to make the best of their abilities. By doing their best, they played serious roles in the history unfolding around them. Sometimes they opened doors, brought new ideas to life, and served as role models for others. Often, they broke the barriers that separated women's spheres from those of men. Women and men today have more choices because of women like them.

Although the four women in this book were extraordinary, for every story told, thousands have been lost. Historians—our culture's "memory keepers"—have always been interested in business, government, politics, and war, and they have written primarily of the men who became prominent in these activities. Women usually worked at home, caring for family and running the household. In the absence of written records about them, it is difficult to document women's contributions or to determine their power and influence.

In traditional oral cultures, like those of Native Americans and African Americans, stories of extraordinary women were told to generation after generation. Yet when those oral traditions disappear, so do the stories. Many women did brave things, but we can only guess at their achievements or the source of their courage.

For researchers, looking at history through the eyes of women is a challenging and exhilarating opportunity to solve mysteries. We sought our women in biographies, family records, and newspapers, always looking for the unrecorded point of view, always wondering, "What did *she* think?" As we worked, we found more and more answers to our questions.

Some accounts in this volume were available only because these women were companions of successful men who left extensive records. We learned that even when a woman was very successful, as in the case of Nell Donnelly Reed, her story was likely to be forgotten. We finally found extensive records of Nell's business filed in an archive under the name of the man she married after building her multi-million-dollar fashion empire.

While it is frustrating that individual life stories are lost, it is much sadder that the stories of entire civilizations have disappeared. Among the earliest known peoples occupying present-day Missouri, well established here when the first European explorers arrived, were the Osage and Missouri nations. Theirs was a complex, successful society that had lasted thousands of years. Native American women had important roles in the daily life of the community. They worked at raising, gathering, and preserving food. They cared for children and passed traditions from elders to young ones. Their skills made them valuable to their people, and their knowledge made them valuable to European explorers.

The first biography in this book traces the life of a Native American woman the French newspapers called "Ignon Ouaconisen," and the people of Paris called "the Missouri Princess." She lived from about 1700 to after 1751, the last date we hear of her. She traveled with the adventurer Etienne de Bourgmont and bore his child, whom he called "Petit Missouri." While much of her story is a mystery, we still know more about her than about other women of the Missouris.

The pioneer Olive Boone, who lived from 1783 to 1858, came to the Louisiana Territory as a sixteen-year-old bride with her husband, Nathan Boone. She guided a skiff and their swimming horses across the Missouri River to join Nathan's relatives near St. Charles. Family records and oral histories show that Olive was independent and resourceful. For much of her married life, she stayed alone with her children and the family slaves while Nathan traveled on hunting, surveying, and military expeditions that took him many miles away. Left on her own for months at a time, Olive survived the toughest of circumstances using only the raw materials available in the rough Missouri wilderness.

In some cases, women showed physical and moral bravery beyond measure. Martha Jane Chisley, born a slave in 1833, was brought to northeast Missouri as a young woman. Brought up a Catholic, she married Peter Paul Tolton, a slave of a neighboring farmer, in the Catholic church at Brush Creek near Monroe City, and their three children were baptized in that church. During the Civil War, Martha Jane escaped with her children to Illinois. She overcame many obstacles, persevering until her son Augustine was able to enter school and get an education. Her son later studied in Rome and became the first nationally known African American priest.

Nell Donnelly of Kansas City was a pioneering business-woman who founded the world's largest dress company, bright-ening the wardrobe of the "housewife" of her day and at the same time creating fair working conditions for her employees. Born into an ordinary middle-class family in 1889, the twelfth of thirteen children of an Irish immigrant father, she achieved a level of celebrity that brought its own problems. During the worst of the Great Depression in 1931, Nell and her chauffeur were kidnapped and held for ransom. The kidnappers threatened to blind her and kill her driver; they might have carried out the threat if her close friend, Senator James Reed, had not managed to intercede with powerful political connections in Kansas City. Nell later married Senator Reed, but long before she was Nell Donnelly Reed she had proven that a woman could establish and run a successful business without heartlessly exploiting those employees who helped make her success.

Each of the women in this book called on her courage, in difficult circumstances, and they all share other characteristics as well. Endurance is a quality many women share. "The longer a race—on land, water, or ice—the better women perform," wrote Dianne Hales in her book, *Just Like a Woman.*

As evidence, Hales reminds us that the world's record for swimming the English Channel was set by a woman, Penny Dean, in 1978. Another woman, Ann Trason, ran a twenty-four-hour race, logging 143 miles, four miles farther than the man who was her closest competitor. Libby Riddles won the grueling Alaska Iditerod in 1985 and Susan Butcher won in 1986, 1987, 1988, and 1990. Shannon Lucid holds the U.S. record for time spent in space: 188 consecutive days. That special gift of endurance often turns out to be the key to success.

In writing this book, we have focused on the history of the times, the roles of women, the choices available to each, and the way each woman transcended her time. This helped us see that with every generation, we learn more and achieve more. Even today, we are changing the world.

# 1

## Ignon Ouaconisen, or "Françoise of the Missouri Nation"

Come! Arise and depart at once. The master of life will have pity on you. We are going to mourn for you for a moment, that we may think of you no more if you die on your journey . . .

—the Great Chief of the Missouri on November 19, 1724,
sending his daughter with Bourgmont to Paris
(quoted by M. M. Quaife)

We will never know her complete story. Like millions of other Native Americans who lived before European settlement, most of her life is a mystery.

She was born around 1700, the daughter of a powerful man of the Missouri Indian nation. In 1724, *Mercure de France,* a newspaper of Paris, France, gave us one of the names we have for her: Ignon Ouaconisen.

Even using the word *Missouri* shows how little we know about her people. *Missouri* was not the name they called themselves, but the name given to them by the French explorer and Jesuit priest Father Jacques Marquette on his 1673 voyage down the Mississippi River with the Canadian trader Louis Jolliet. Marquette and Jolliet had reached the Mississippi from a remote mission in present-day Michigan, traveling in birchbark canoes with five

5

Native American guides and rowers from the Illinois branch of the Algonquian family of tribes.

According to the linguist Donald M. Lance, who has studied the origin of the word *Missouri,* the explorers stopped to visit the Peoria tribes and asked them about the people farther down the river.

The Peorias replied with a term that sounded like "ouemissourit," which in their language meant "people with big canoes." This was not the name of the people, but a description based on the tribe's dugout canoes, carved from the giant cottonwood trees that grew along the river. Missouri canoes could carry as many as twelve people with gear, making them much larger than the Illinois birchbark canoes, which carried two or three people.

Marquette wrote "ouemissourit" on his map, the first known map of the region. Later explorers adopted the name for the people and eventually for the river. Over the years, it became standardized as *Missouri.*

According to Michael J. O'Brien and W. Raymond Wood in *The Prehistory of Missouri,* the Missouri people had migrated to the Missouri River area in the 1500s, settling in villages near the confluence of the Grand and Missouri Rivers. In those days, the hills were covered with a wooded forest of tall oak and hickory trees sheltering a diverse population of animals and woodland plants. Transportation was by canoe or on paths shared by humans and animals. Wild berries, nuts, mushrooms, and other foods ripened in their seasons for people to gather and store.

The French adventurer Etienne de Bourgmont was one of the first Europeans to explore and write about the area, and in 1714 he described his journey on the Mississippi and Missouri Rivers in his *Exact Description of Louisiana, of Its Harbors, Lands and Rivers, and Names of the Indian Tribes That Occupy It, and the Commerce and Advantages to Be Derived Therefrom for the Establishment of a Colony.*

Swiss painter Karl Bodmer drew this Missouri man when he traveled up the Missouri River in 1833, more than a century after the tribe had moved from its homeland. Archaeologist Bob Bray has noted this man's "slightly downcast appearance" and described his hair and ornaments: "[it] is arranged with a sort of modified roach. . . . All the hair was cut or plucked over all the scalp except that in a narrow band beginning near the top of the head and extending to near the nape of the neck. . . . The ears are distended and festooned with strings of numerous beads, some shaped like . . . cones or spangles of copper. . . . Several strands of beads encircle the neck." Bray believed that most Missouris were around five feet tall. (State Historical Society of Missouri, Columbia.)

The report mentions tribes that are friendly to the French, but Bourgmont wrote almost nothing about the lives of the people or their culture. Instead, he recorded the location of resources such as good land, water, and minerals that might be valuable and the names of chiefs who might be helpful. About the Missouri, he said, "They are of very good blood and are more alert than any other tribe. From the Missouri's River can be gotten furs of every kind, very fine and good, as the climate there is very cold."

We have little direct information about the lives of any Missouri women at this time, including that of Ignon Ouaconisen, but by bringing together the information in early journals and writings of Bourgmont's associates, the Paris newspaper reports of the time, and the research of archaeologists, we can learn something of the life of this daughter of the Great Chief of the Missouri.

In the early 1700s, the Missouri village occupied a site south of the Missouri River in present-day Saline County. Today, part of the village site is in Van Meter State Park, near Miami, Missouri. From their village on interlocking ridges above the river valley, the Missouri could control transportation on the river. The waterways were also a rich source of valuable aquatic plants and animals. Near the village, woodlands buffered the harsh winds, and clear springs provided drinking water.

Archaeologists—scientists who study historic and prehistoric peoples by digging for the things they left behind—have excavated many items the Indians used. Archaeologist Carl Chapman told a *Kansas City Star* reporter in 1956 that the Missouri village was "so rich in clues to the way of life of the Missouri tribe . . . that it may one day be a showplace."

A team of archaeologists led by Robert T. Bray excavated part of the Missouri village. In an article in the *Missouri Historical Review* of April 1961, Bray estimated that in 1703 there were a thousand or more Missouri families in the area. In their book *Indians and Archaeology of Missouri*, Carl and Eleanor Chapman described the Missouri as "numerous and powerful, the first and strongest to be met when traveling up the Missouri River."

In 1991, Bray wrote that radiocarbon dating showed that the site, called the Utz site by the archaeologists, was occupied as early as 1450. He also believed that it had been abandoned about 1712. This conclusion was based partly on the fact that the archaeologists found very few European trade items. However, even though he worked there many years, with help of students from the University of Missouri–Columbia, Bray was only able to excavate a small patch of the entire site.

The Missouri moved frequently, and their homes were constructed for short-term use. Bray reported that when they left the site about 1712, they moved a few miles up the river to another place, now called Gumbo Point, where they lived until about 1727, when they moved still farther up the river. Their migrations make it hard to say with authority exactly where they lived during the span of our story.

The Missouri people were related to the Oto and the Ioway, who lived on the western plains, in present-day Kansas, Iowa, and Nebraska. They traded with other groups and used natural resources from many areas. They chipped flint stone into arrowheads. "The Missouri were accomplished potters, and fragments of their many vessels are among the most common finds," according to Bray. They shaped clay into jars and hardened them in the fire. The jars, beautifully shaped and incised, and sometimes made with handles, made it possible to carry water and store foods.

Bray found arrowheads chipped from flint at the village site, along with other tools: "the stone mortar and pestle for grinding corn and seeds and for crushing mineral paints; the bone awl, punch, and needle . . . hoes made from bison shoulder blades; and various other items." A spoon was made with a clam shell fitted in a deer bone for a handle. The bone had been carved with a slot so the shell fit snugly. Bray also found conch shells from the Gulf of Mexico and red pipestone from Minnesota, suggesting that the Missouri traveled the rivers to trade with Native Americans from miles away.

According to Bray, and later affirmed by Michael O'Brien and Raymond Wood in *The Prehistory of Missouri,* the villagers lived in oval wigwams made with long, slender poles covered with animal skins and perhaps woven mats. The poles were shoved into the ground at one end, then "bent together and tied at the top to produce an elongated domed frame." The large wigwams measured about fifteen by seven meters—or up to fifty feet long. Because few of them had fireplaces, Bray speculated that the village was not used in winter, but, as we have noted, nothing about the Missouri is certain. Some of the house interiors seemed carefully tended, and others were not. "It is reasonable to say the people were relatively good housekeepers," Bray wrote, "but different households had different views of aesthetics."

It seemed that the houses had zones for certain activities, such as milling or toolmaking. This might mean that there were men's areas and women's areas, but archaeologists are not sure. There is also a question of how the Missouri decided exactly where to build their homes. Because Bray found that some houses were built on the site of earlier houses, and even over graves or trash pits, he concluded that the village was periodically abandoned, then resettled. However, they buried their dead nearby, sometimes close to their homes.

The durable system of Native American life had been evolving for at least ten thousand years. Skills had been handed down from generation to generation; children learned by watching and helping. Tribes preserved their history and culture by demonstration and storytelling. Both men and women gained the practical knowledge that enabled them to survive.

A Missouri girl would have grown up mostly with her mother's family, with aunts, sisters, and grandmothers in the household.

Clothing was very simple and practical. As a young child, she probably went naked or wrapped simply in a soft animal skin, even in cold weather. At age six or seven, she would have begun to wear clothing that was much like that of the adults—moccasins, leggings, skirts, and long tunics, all made from soft leathers. As an unmarried woman, she would have worn her hair in a long braid, perhaps tied and decorated with shells and feathers.

Girls learned at an early age to help with planting, preserving, and preparing food. The Native American diet was in large part vegetarian, and most was provided by the women. One spring ritual for Missouri women was gathering the American lotus for its edible seeds and roots. Also in the spring, the women started gardens of pumpkin, beans, and corn while the young men practiced their hunting skills. As summer approached, the villagers took the mats and animal skins from the large wigwams and walked to the plains for bison hunting season. The mats and skins would be used to cover tepees as they camped along the way.

The hunters, men at the peak of their strength, ran ahead and killed game such as turkey, deer, bear, and elk to feed the others. Following the hunters came the women, older men, and boys and girls carrying tools, food, and supplies. Traveling with this group, a girl would learn from her elders where to find plants to gather for food and medicine. One of Etienne de Bourgmont's men, watching the families travel, wrote that "Girls of ten or twelve years carry at least 100 pounds—but it is true they can carry such a load for only two or three leagues." Since a league is 2.76 U.S. miles, this amounted to five to eight miles carrying a heavy load.

If drought had killed the prairie grass, the families had to walk a long way to find bison—sometimes as far as two hundred miles. In average years, the bison roamed the prairie in herds of thousands. Bourgmont described the prairies as "the most beautiful country and the most beautiful pieces of land in the

The *travois,* a Canadian French term, was described carefully by Bourg-mont's journal keeper. Men put a leather harness on the dog and attached "two large poles, the thickness of a man's arm and about 12 feet long" to carry the load. "One dog drags the skins to make a shelter big enough to sleep 10 or 12 persons, along with their dishes, pots, and other utensils, weighing around 300 pounds." (State Historical Society of Missouri, Columbia.)

world . . . like the seas and full of wild beasts, especially buffalo, cows, hind and stags, which are there in such numbers that stagger the imagination."

Bourgmont reported that the Kansa hunted with bow and arrow, and the same could have been said of the Missouri. During the hunt, families, including the children, worked as a team to surround the animals.

When a bison kill was made, everyone helped prepare the carcass; every part of the animal had a use. Some parts were a delicacy to eat right away. Other parts were cut into strips and dried for winter. Bones were made into tools. The skin made a valuable blanket or a covering for a house. Sinews—the stringy parts that work the joints—were used for sewing. Families preserved the

*Chasse Générale au Boeuf.*
*mais a pied .*

This 1758 illustration was published in France to show how the Indians hunted on foot, surrounding the herd. The hunters killed only as many animals as they needed, so buffalo were usually plentiful before European settlement. (State Historical Society of Missouri, Columbia.)

meat in the sun. Nothing was wasted—bones, horn, skin, sinew, and meat were cleaned and preserved.

Their packs were heavy on the walk home. In their untended gardens, pumpkins, beans, and corn would be ready to harvest. Years of experience had taught them to plant these three essential crops so that they nourished each other. The cornstalks grow tall and provide support for the climbing bean plants. Bean roots add nitrogen, a valuable corn fertilizer, to the soil. Pumpkin vines creep along the ground, shading all the roots and protecting the topsoil.

Their gardens also hosted a good many unexpected plants that we might today call weeds. The Missouri people would have used some of those wild plants for food or medicine.

In the autumn forest, there were nuts and berries to gather and preserve. Acorns were especially prized but required time-consuming processing before they could become a useful flour. Foods for the winter were packed into clay pots and lowered into storage pits—hand-dug holes so deep a person could stand in them.

In the early 1700s, the French claimed the Mississippi River valley and set up trading posts on the river. The explorer René-Robert, sieur de La Salle, had reached the Gulf of Mexico and claimed the region for King Louis XIV of France in April 1682. La Salle took possession in the name of his king to all of the land on both sides of the Mississippi River, "all the nations, people, provinces, cities, towns, villages, mines, minerals, fisheries, streams, and rivers." He called the territory Louisiana for his king, Louis XIV.

The French thought of the inhabitants of the region as part of their property. The French word *sauvage* means a person untouched by "civilization," and the early French explorers felt responsible for converting Native Americans to Christianity. According to La Salle's notary, in a report signed by La Salle himself and others in the company, the explorer ordered a cross raised near the mouth of the Mississippi. He reminded his party that "his Majesty, as eldest Son of the Church, would annex no country without making it his chief care to establish the Christian religion."

Later in the seventeenth and eighteenth centuries, as Europeans read the reports about Native American life sent home by explorers, missionaries, and travelers in the New World, the image of the Native American as a "free man in Nature," a "noble

The Missouri dug deep holes to store clay jars of dried corn, acorns, beans, and other foods for winter use. Bob Bray found that the floors were lined with grass and the walls were carefully finished with smooth clay. Digging such a pit using shovels made of buffalo bone would be hard work, and the pits must have been in use for years; eventually, however, they were abandoned and filled with dirt and debris. These trash pits became treasure troves for archaeologists, who found in them pieces of pottery, broken tools, animal bones, and even an occasional human bone. (Drawing from Carl H. Chapman and Eleanor F. Chapman, *Indians and Archaeology of Missouri, Revised Edition* [Columbia: University of Missouri Press, 1983].)

savage," developed. A Jesuit missionary in Canada wrote, "we see in the savages the fine remains of human nature [which is] entirely corrupted among civilized people." In the early 1730s, the English poet Alexander Pope wrote in his *Essay on Man* of the

> Indian whose untutor'd mind
> Sees God in clouds, or hears him on the wind;
> His soul, proud science never taught to stray.

The French philosopher Jean-Jacques Rousseau first used the term *noble savage* in his *Discourse on the Origins of Inequality among Mankind,* published in 1755 and widely circulated throughout Europe. The idea was expressed in poetry, painting, statues, wall hangings, and philosophical works throughout the century and led many Europeans to measure their own existence and the behavior of their rulers and royal families against life in the natural world of the Indians.

Meanwhile, explorers traveling up the Mississippi and Missouri Rivers recognized that the Indian tribes would make eager trading partners. European rulers were hungry for treasure from the New World. In return for manufactured goods such as glass beads and shiny medals with images of their king, Native American hunters could provide deer and beaver skins and other goods to sell in Europe.

European trade had changed Missouri life as early as 1683, when La Salle noted there were two Frenchmen living among the Missouri. In 1684, a traveler reported that the Missouri owned horses, which they used to carry packs. Horses had come to the New World with the Spanish in the 1500s. By 1704, according to Jean Baptiste Le Moyne de Bienville, the governor of French Louisiana, there were 110 French traders along the Mississippi and Missouri Rivers, working individually or in groups of seven or eight men.

The French often took Native American women as guides and companions. The women could translate when meeting other Native Americans, and they could show the explorers how to use native plants and where to hunt and trap.

These were skills they had practiced from childhood. When a girl reached age twelve, she was expected to do her share of work. She helped care for younger children. She knew how to sew skins, how to help hunt, and how to preserve plants and meat. By the time she was old enough to menstruate—at about age fourteen in those days—her father would have already found a husband for her. Under normal circumstances, this would have been a man from another family of the Missouri nation, but the life of the "Missouri princess" was to become entwined with the life of a tall, mysterious French explorer.

Far away, Etienne de Bourgmont was living near present-day Detroit, Michigan. Bourgmont was born in 1679 in central Normandy and came to Canada about 1698 as a soldier in the French army. French officials in Quebec sent him to Detroit in 1705, but at heart Bourgmont was more adventurer than soldier. He deserted his post in 1706 and one observer wrote that he was "living in the woods like a savage," an "outlaw bushranger" engaged in illegal fur trade.

In 1712, the Sac and Fox Indians attacked the French fort near Detroit. Other Native Americans, from nations that traded with the French, traveled to defend the fort. The Missouri, Osage, and Illinois entered the battle on the side of the French. In the Native American tradition, the Missouri had taken all their village members to the fort, including women and children. Some historians believe that Bourgmont saw the beautiful young woman then, and fell in love.

It is also possible that he was pursuing business interests, because the French government was just beginning to allow private investors to trade with the Native Americans. We will never know the truth, but Bourgmont joined the Missouri in their village

Carl and Eleanor Chapman described the spring ritual of gathering lotus roots: "The women, young and old, dug the lily roots from the shallow lakes, using long, pointed poles. Much ceremony accompanied the collecting of the first root, and part of it was carefully returned to the water" so that the plants could grow back. The Chapmans called the gathering "an occasion of gaiety and frolic." (Drawing from Carl H. Chapman and Eleanor F. Chapman, *Indians and Archaeology of Missouri, Revised Edition.*)

about 1712, either at the Utz site or the new location a few miles upriver.

In terms of today's society, we cannot really compare the relationship between Bourgmont and the young Missouri woman with relationships today. While Native American women had skills and much knowledge, the group's very survival depended on obedience, cooperation, and the hard work of all members. Children paid attention to their elders. A young Missouri woman might have been thinking about love and marriage, but she would have been waiting for her family to plan her future.

Certainly her father would have arranged the meetings between Bourgmont and his daughter. Perhaps he saw a chance to make a powerful French friend. Perhaps he gave his daughter to Bourgmont as a gesture of respect. The Osage historian John Joseph Mathews reports that the Missouri "allowed each trader or trapper . . . to stay and even gave them their most beautiful women." Bourgmont might have given gifts to the chief in exchange for the young woman, as was the custom.

We also have no way of knowing exactly how old she was when she met the French explorer, but historians believe she was probably about twelve or thirteen. Bourgmont used the Missouri village as a base while he explored other areas. The next spring, he traveled farther, taking the young woman with him. For a time, according to Bourgmont biographer Frank Norall, two other Frenchmen and their Indian companions went along.

By 1714, Bourgmont had well-established ties with the Missouri and had explored the region and filed his *Exact Description of Louisiana.* His years of traveling among the Indians had been reported by other French explorers as "scandalous, even criminal." He soon came to the notice of priests and military commanders in Illinois, and word of his activities reached Quebec and all the way to France, to King Louis XIV living at the royal residence in Versailles.

In spite of his "scandalous, even criminal" reputation, Bourgmont's knowledge about Native Americans was valuable to the French, who wanted to develop the fur trade. Missouri beaver and deer skins were valued in Europe and could be exchanged for manufactured items. Later, rifles and black powder would become part of the trade.

In 1714, the young Missouri girl had a baby boy. Bourgmont began to take "Petit Missouri" or "Little Missouri" with him on his travels as soon as the child could leave his mother. No doubt, the boy's presence was responsible in part for the great affection the Missouri people held for Bourgmont. In 1720, when Petit Missouri was only five years old, Bourgmont took the boy to France. He promised the Missouri and other tribes that he would return.

The young mother might have thought that she would never see them again. Several years passed. Louis XIV had died in 1715, and his great grandson Louis XV, who was only five years old, succeeded to the throne. Philip, Duke of Orleans, ruled in the child's place as regent. The new French regime wanted to secure the Missouri River and hold the lands to the west by building a French fort on the river, a plan that Governor Bienville strongly supported, fearing the Spanish had designs on the Mississippi Valley.

Bourgmont had been recommended for the job by the French commandant at Kaskaskia, who said that "He had great influence over the Indians when he was there. They demand him back with eagerness on every occasion." The Osage historian John Joseph Mathews wrote that Bourgmont was among the few men of "conscience and humanity" that lived among the Indians in Missouri. His "conscience and humanity," along with the fact that he had a half-Indian son, would bring him back to Missouri.

Bourgmont might have been happy to stay in France. He had been commissioned as the commandant of the Missouri River and had been made a knight of the Order of the Cross of St. Louis. Even though he was raising Petit Missouri, he did not consider his relationship with the child's mother to be a marriage. In fact, while at home, the forty-one-year-old Bourgmont had married a wealthy twenty-nine-year-old Frenchwoman and fathered a daughter.

Still, the prospect of returning to the Missouri appealed to him. In addition to establishing the fort, the French wanted him to explore farther west. They also asked him to bring a delegation of Indians back to Paris to meet the court "in order to give them an idea of the power of the French." When these things were accomplished, he would receive a royal title that would ensure a comfortable life for his French family.

In the 1720s, the trip from France to the New World took more than three months, and when Bourgmont with Petit Missouri and his few men arrived in the port of New Orleans on the Mississippi River, they learned that the orders to prepare for his journey upriver could not be filled. Since Bourgmont had left, the situation had worsened: An economic collapse, a famine, and a hurricane had caused such hardship that Bienville's interest in a fort on the Missouri River had faded. Even orders from France could not produce men, boats, and supplies.

Finally, Bourgmont found three barges, rowers, and several pirogues, a type of canoe. They hoped to find more men and supplies as they rowed up the Mississippi River, but settlements were few and far between, and supplies were short. On the way, the rowers deserted, and most of the soldiers were afflicted with fever and malnutrition.

When Bourgmont and his crew neared the mouth of the Missouri above St. Louis, however, they were delighted to see the Missouri people waiting. Petit Missouri's mother was probably among the welcoming group. The child had become a nine-year-old. The Missouri families joyfully greeted their old friend Bourgmont and took him and his fifteen men back to the village.

Bourgmont and his men decided to build Fort Orleans across from the Missouri village, on the north side of the river, in what

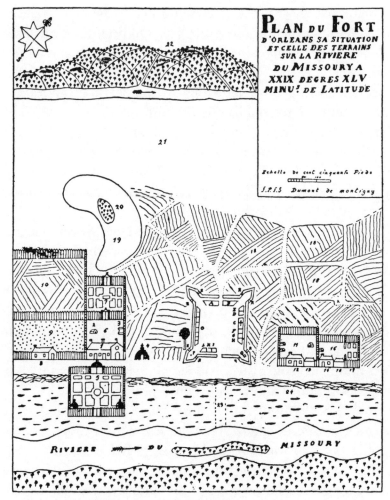

Only a few buildings and small enclosures were ever completed at Fort Orleans, but this plan shows that a high fence, or stockade, was to surround the fort to protect the soldiers and the Native American traders. Within the stockade, there were to be areas for trading, meeting, weapon storage, soldier barracks, and worship. Agricultural fields would supply food and pasture. In this plan, two sentries would watch the river from the corners of the fenced reception area. (State Historical Society of Missouri, Columbia.)

is today Carroll County. As the fort took shape, the Missouri and the French worked together. They built the structures with upright logs, a building technique different from most American cabins, which had logs notched at the ends and laid horizontally. The French securely buried the ends of logs in the ground, close together to protect the fort from attack. The roofs were thatched with grass cut and prepared by the Missouri women.

Petit Missouri might have stayed with Bourgmont, or he might have joined his Missouri relatives to learn to shoot arrows and hunt. His mother most likely visited the fort, watching the French-style log buildings take shape or helping gather the thatch. One of the men, a Sergeant Du Bois, who would stay with Bourgmont throughout the visit, was later to become a significant part of her life.

The men built a warehouse for ammunition, a chapel, a house for the chaplain, and then Bourgmont's own house. Because of the small crew and the intense labor required, progress was slow. Two of his lieutenants made complaints against him, and Bourgmont complained in a letter that the men would not make "a little fence to provide cover for five pigs and twenty chickens" intended to supply eggs and meat if people were trapped inside during an enemy attack.

In June 1724, Bourgmont decided to take his trip west. A journal keeper, who was perhaps the engineer who accompanied him, made careful records, noting that Bourgmont took nine men and one hundred Missouri including "eight war chiefs and the head chief of the tribe, and 64 Osages commanded by four war chiefs of their tribe." The report does not mention any woman specifically, but women would have been in the party.

It was almost midsummer and the days were long. The travelers tried to keep a strict schedule, moving across the land in military style, following a compass west-southwest, and in time to a drummer. They left camp by four in the morning, walked until midmorning, rested through the heat of the day until midafternoon, and then marched until dusk, when they made camp. They covered about six leagues, or fifteen miles, per day. The Indians went ahead, killing game for food—about ten deer each day and several turkeys.

Twenty-three of Bourgmont's men traveled by water in pirogues loaded with gifts while Bourgmont and his group went overland. While they camped near a Kansa Indian village to wait for the pirogues, chiefs brought peace pipes to them.

They spread a bison robe and put Bourgmont on it, carrying him to the head chief. The Indians gathered around and stroked him, a sign of great affection and respect. A journal kept by one of Bourgmont's men records the Kansa greeting: "You have crossed the Great Lake [the Atlantic Ocean]. You promised to return; you have kept your word to us. Thus, we love you."

The Kansa insisted that the explorers stay for ten days of feasting and celebration. They offered Bourgmont "the head chief's daughter, 13 or 14 years old . . . that he may marry her," but Bourgmont told them he was already married and that Frenchmen could not have two wives. The Kansa then insisted that the girl should be married to Petit Missouri when he was old enough. "We give her to your son . . . he will be our head chief and you will be truly our father." Bourgmont replied that he would let Petit Missouri decide for himself when he was older, and the Indians agreed to keep the girl until that time.

The Kansa had brought horses and Native American slaves from other tribes to trade with Bourgmont for manufactured goods, including gunpowder, gunshot, beads, and knives. Two of the slaves were members of the Padouca, or Plains Apache, western tribes that Bourgmont planned to visit. Bourgmont wanted them "for the express purpose of returning them to their tribe," to show that the French were there to make peace.

During the visit with the Kansa, many of the Missouri became ill with fever. Bourgmont had to act as a doctor and prepare medicines. He had observed in his early report that the Indians had valuable plants they used for medicines. He also resorted to a common cure of the time and "bled" the patients. Many of the sick got better.

Finally, the pirogues arrived and Bourgmont gave the Kansa chiefs a pile of gifts equal in size to a pile they had given to him. By the time he left the Kansa village, as one of his men recorded, the procession had grown to nineteen Frenchmen, two head chiefs, fourteen war chiefs, three hundred Indian warriors and as many women, five hundred children, and three hundred dogs. Horses carried some of the supplies.

About sixty leagues from the Padouca village, Bourgmont was overcome with fever. He could not get on his horse and had to return with his party to Fort Orleans by pirogue. The large group of Native Americans accompanying him dispersed, going to their homes or hunting grounds. A small group, including the Padouca slaves from the western tribes, continued west with the gifts. Bourgmont later received word that their families had received them with great joy.

In the autumn, Bourgmont started out again, and this time he was able to reach the nations to the west. His return of the slaves, his reputation, and his skill with the Indians gave him power over them. "For me, with the Indians nothing is impossible," he wrote. Bourgmont's journal keeper described women who brought plates of cooked meat, sun-dried meat, pounded meat, fruits, and corn. "It was all they had in the villages. In a word, one could hardly believe all the attentions these people showered upon us during our stay with them."

Having built the fort and made peace with the nations to the west, Bourgmont's final task was to take a delegation of Native Americans to France. The record of the council meeting of the Missouri is preserved in the French national archives. They offered to send "four chiefs . . . and the daughter of the head chief of our tribe, so that you may conduct them to the country which is the source of our fusils [flintlock rifles], gunpowder, and generally all the merchandise that we have."

The French newspaper *Mercure de France* reported that the "daughter of the head chief" was indeed the mother of Petit Missouri, and that she "passed as [Bourgmont's] mistress." She would have been about twenty-five years old. The *Mercure* called her Ignon Ouaconisen.

In saying good-bye, her father had spoken to Bourgmont of Petit Missouri, saying, "One of our children has been there and is returning to us" and told him, "You have never deceived us. Take care of your children. If they do not return within twenty-five moons, we shall account them dead."

Bourgmont, Du Bois, and the Native Americans began the thousand-mile trip from Fort Orleans to New Orleans in November 1724. The *Mercure* reported that Bourgmont had set out with "fifteen or sixteen Savages from the different Missouri nations" and four from the Illinois. A Jesuit priest completed the party.

They arrived in New Orleans on January 9, 1725, and waited for the first sailing ship to France. The historian Frank Norall says that the expense of keeping so many in port and paying their passage was too much, so most of the Native Americans were sent back to their homes. According to his account, in February or March, four chiefs, Ignon Ouaconisen, Bourgmont, and Du Bois boarded the sailing ship *La Bellone*. Also on board was all their baggage, including their finest clothing, and gifts for the French royalty.

The trip across the Atlantic on a sailing ship was dangerous even with the best of luck. Leaving New Orleans, *La Bellone* struck floating logs and a sandbar. The rudder was damaged. While stopped at Dauphine Island, the ship suddenly burst open and sank. Six sailors died, and the entire cargo was lost. Now the group had only the clothes they were wearing, and they had to wait for another ship.

In its account of the story, the *Mercure* reported that more Native Americans had been ready to board the ship for the voyage, but when they saw it sink, they "lost courage and turned back for home."

The "Missouri princess," Bourgmont, Du Bois, four chiefs, and the priest finally crossed the ocean in a ship called *La Gironde*. The four chiefs were members of four tribes: the Missouri, the Osage, the Oto, and the Illinois. On the voyage, there were new dangers. Besides the threat of shipwreck and drowning, diseases such as malaria and scurvy were constant threats. One chief died at sea. The others arrived in Paris safely, after ten months of travel, on September 20, 1725.

The Parisians were intensely curious about the Indians. To them America was a vast new world of wild places and wild people, and some considered the Native Americans to be childlike, virtuous "noble savages," uncorrupted by European civilization. The *Mercure* described their first public appearance; they were "in the ceremonial costume of their country . . . utterly nude but with all of their body daubed with different colors and with a feather head-piece and . . . a red loin cloth attached to a belt." They carried bows and arrows and a huge calumet, or peace pipe, that was hung with feathers. Their appearance no doubt confirmed French opinion that Native Americans were in need of Christian teaching.

Two of the chiefs made formal speeches to the French court. Menspere, the Missouri chief, spoke on behalf of his nation as well as the Osage and Oto. Chief Chicagou spoke for his people, the Illinois, saying, "Even though I am Chief in my own village and well-regarded within my own nation, I am nothing . . . but I love prayer and the French. Thus you should love me and my Nation, which has always been allied with the French." He also asked the French not to push the Native Americans out of the lands "where we have placed our hearths." Their speeches were reported by the *Mercure*.

After the formal speeches, each visitor received a gift of clothing. For the men, "a complete outfit of clothing in the French style: a blue dress coat with silver ornaments and buttons, a red jacket trimmed in silver, red knee-breeches and stockings, a plumed hat trimmed with silver, six elaborate shirts, six collars, etc."

Ignon Ouaconisen, called the "Savagesse," received a "flame-colored linen dress with a design of gold flowers, a petticoat of the same material along with a hoop petticoat, two corsets, six fine blouses, six pairs of puffed sleeves, but no other ornaments because she always went bare-headed." Gold and silver ribbons and silk stockings completed her outfit.

The Parisians took the visitors on a grand tour of the city. They were interested to see the "great copper vats and roasting spits" at the Hotel des Invalides, a military hospital, and "asked if there were enough warriors to eat all the meat." They enjoyed a performance of an opera and the elaborate gardens and fountains at Versailles. The *Mercure* reported: "Their astonishment at the beauty of the things they had seen was inexpressible . . . they wanted to know how the animals and birds could spout water through their mouths."

The group met King Louis XV, who was then fifteen years old. He took the men on a hunt and gave each visitor a royal medallion on a gold chain, a rifle, a game bag, a sword, a watch, and a painting "depicting the audience that they had with the King." The "Missouri princess" became a Catholic in a baptism at the Cathedral of Notre Dame and married Sergeant Du Bois in a Catholic ceremony.

We can imagine her bewilderment at the service. Perhaps her gaze rested first on her own elegant dress with its hoop skirt, then on the massive carved stone pillars of the cathedral, the solemn priest in his black gown and white collar, and finally, the military man next to her. The Latin mass would have echoed off the stone walls and the high stone ceiling. The crisp autumn air would have been heavily perfumed with incense.

She had come from half a world away on a ship that, for all its size, was tossed on the ocean like a feather; she had been looked at, showered with gifts, fussed over, and given strange foods to eat. In contrast to spoons made from shell and deer bone, she had eaten with spoons of silver. Did she understand the meaning of the wedding ceremony, so strange to a young woman from a Native American family? As with so many mysteries in her life, we will never know.

The church marriage would have, of course, given her a proper relationship with Du Bois in the eyes of the French. It also relieved Bourgmont of any obligation to her. He was given the title of squire and designed for himself a coat of arms. It had "on [an] azure background, a naked savage reclining on a mountain of silver."

Du Bois, his Missouri bride, and the chiefs stayed in Paris about two months and enjoyed a final party on November 28. They then sailed from France and arrived safely back in the New World. They planned to travel back up the Mississippi River to take the chiefs back home. Here, the story breaks off. One historian reports that in an ambush on the way up the Mississippi, Du Bois disappeared. He might have died there. Another historian believes that the couple returned to Ignon Ouaconisen's people and that Du Bois died in an attack on Fort Orleans.

Eventually, the "Missouri princess" settled in Kaskaskia, Illinois, a French village founded by Catholic missionaries in 1675 on the east bank of the Mississippi River where she was known as "Françoise of the Missouri Nation." She married a captain of the militia named Marin and had one or two children with him.

Kaskaskia, according to one visitor, had about four hundred inhabitants by 1724: "very good people . . . They have a very pretty church, there are about 20 French voyageurs [men with

Ignon Ouaconisen returns home with her husband in one of many murals in the Missouri State Capitol. In this idealized image, the artist shows Ignon Ouaconisen in a white, European-style wedding dress and bonnet. Du Bois is at her side, and her Native American family is gathered around them. (Walker-Missouri Resources Division, courtesy State Historical Society of Missouri, Columbia.)

licenses to acquire boats and trade goods] who settled there and married Indian women . . . they grow wheat and have inspired the Indians to grow some, from which they find much pleasure in eating French bread."

In 1741, a 650-pound bell, a gift from King Louis XV, came to Kaskaskia. The bell was transported by ship from France and up the Mississippi River from New Orleans, retracing the path taken by Bourgmont. It was inscribed "For the Church of the Illinois, A Gift of the King from Across the Water." The arrival of the bell and its installation in the church must have brought back many memories for the "Missouri princess."

The last report of her comes from 1752, when a French traveler met her in Kaskaskia. She still had the watch given to her by Louis XV. The traveler wrote that it was a "beautiful repeating watch, which the Indians called a spirit, because its movements seemed to them supernatural."

We know nothing more about that beautiful daughter of a powerful Missouri chief or her children. In the 1880s, Kaskaskia was cut off from the mainland by floods. Much of the town— even the cemetery, grave by grave—was washed away, taking away the answers forever. Kaskaskia is now an island, located closer to Missouri than to Illinois.

Fort Orleans was abandoned in 1728. By this time, war and disease brought by the Europeans had ravaged the Native Americans. The steep decline in population left them vulnerable to attacks from their old enemies, the Sac and Fox. Some Missouri Indians came to the site of St. Louis in 1764 and helped Auguste Chouteau and his men clear it and build a stone fort, but about that time most of the Missouri people dispersed. Some joined the Osage and others went west to join the Oto and Kansa.

The archaeologist Robert T. Bray wrote that the tribe "was reduced to a pitiful remnant of 30 families by 1804" when Lewis and Clark passed what they called the Missouri's "ancient village." Disease and war were two major reasons for the Native Americans' decline, but Bray writes about a third reason: "the general though slow breakdown of tribal customs which resulted from relations with the white man."

Indeed, the courageous Missouri lost their hold on the land around the village. The fur trade declined, and future white settlers wanted to claim land for farming. Many Missouri families ended up in Council Bluffs, Iowa, in a settlement of poor whites and Native Americans from various tribes. By 1841, the Indians had become addicted to liquor, and missionaries in Council Bluffs reported that drunken men and women "wallowed themselves in the mud."

The story of the "Missouri princess," who was called to courage as a young woman, is full of mysteries. If nothing else, her story reveals how little we know about early Native Americans. In the words of Michael J. O'Brien and W. Raymond Wood, authors of *The Prehistory of Missouri,* "Perhaps this is the way all serious inquiry goes—that is, an exercise raises more questions than it provides answers for."

## FOR MORE READING

A summary on Bourgmont's life by Frank Norall is published in the *Dictionary of Missouri Biography,* edited by Lawrence O. Christensen et al. (Columbia: University of Missouri Press, 1999).

A complete biography of Bourgmont's years in the New World is Frank Norall's *Bourgmont: Explorer of the Missouri, 1698–1725* (Lincoln: University of Nebraska Press, 1988). It details many aspects of Bourgmont's life, including his relationship to the Missouri woman. Norall did most of his research at collections in Paris, France.

Carl H. Chapman and Eleanor F. Chapman wrote *Indians and Archaeology of Missouri* (Columbia: University of Missouri Press, 1983). In it they describe their own discoveries and Missouri Indian findings by University of Missouri archaeologist Robert T. Bray.

The most recent book on Missouri tribes is Michael J. O'Brien and W. Raymond Wood's *The Prehistory of Missouri* (Columbia: University of Missouri Press, 2000). It reports on the work of previous archaeologists and adds much from the findings of O'Brien and Wood.

In *Deep River: A Memoir of a Missouri Farm,* David Hamilton, who grew up near the site of the Missouri village, writes of Bourgmont, the "Missouri princess," Petit Missouri, and the land and woods they had known more than two hundred years earlier (Columbia: University of Missouri Press, 2001).

*Detroit Biographies: The Sieur de Bourgmont,* by M. M. Quaife (Burton Historical Collection Leaflets, vol. 6, no. 4, Detroit Public Library, March 1928), unfortunately out of print, focuses on Bourgmont's years in Detroit but includes information about the Missouri.

Kristie Wolferman's book *The Osage in Missouri* (Columbia: University of Missouri Press, 1997) provides a good overview on the Osage, neighbors of the Missouri, and is part of the Missouri Heritage Readers Series.

Other books on the Osage include John Joseph Mathews's *The Osages: Children of the Middle Waters* (1961; reprint, Norman: University of Oklahoma Press, 1982). A more recent study, incorporating newer findings, is *The Osage: An Ethnohistorical Study of Hegemony of the Prairie-Plains,* by Willard H. Rollings (Columbia: University of Missouri Press, 1992).

*The Many Hands of My Relations: French and Indians on the Lower Mississippi,* by Tanis C. Thorne (Columbia: University of Missouri Press, 1996), reports insightfully on Bourgmont's mission to negotiate with the western tribes and cites sources that indicate that the Missouri woman who married Bourgmont had the name "Françoise of the Missouri Nation" when she lived in Kaskaskia.

# 2

## *Olive Vanbibber Boone*

Without any company but my husband, I started to Missouri or Upper Louisiana. We had two ponies and our pack horse. . . . It was rather a perilous way for so young a couple. I was just sixteen, my husband eighteen.

—Olive Boone, to Lyman C. Draper, 1851

Olive Vanbibber was born January 13, 1783, in a house on the Greenbriar River, in Greenbriar County, Virginia. From an early age, she learned the skills necessary to survive on the frontier. Her young life, however, like the lives of most other young women of her time, passed without record.

The recorded events of Olive's life were generally those that involved her husband, Nathan Boone, the youngest son of the legendary frontiersman Daniel Boone. Still, when writing the history of the American frontier, we should take special care that the story of pioneer women is told. Although they have received little notice until recently, pioneer women played a vital role in the survival and success of their families. Sometimes left on her own for long periods of time, and often in harsh weather, a pioneer woman raised livestock, tended crops, hauled water, protected the homestead, and educated her children in the ways of wilderness survival.

A German visitor to the Boone home in 1833 recorded that "Mrs. Boone, in spite of the many hardships she has experienced, is still a good-looking lady. With her pretty daughters she was busily embroidering artful blankets. Her whole demeanor and the whole demeanor of these ladies would not at all be inappropriate for any German city lady." (State Historical Society of Missouri, Columbia.)

In over fifty-seven years of marriage to Olive, Nathan spent more than a dozen years exploring and soldiering away from home. In this portrait, Nathan wears his military uniform. Nathan's business and pioneer adventures would have been impossible without his resourceful wife. (State Historical Society of Missouri, Columbia.)

A woman cared for her husband and relatives when they were sick or growing old. Olive Boone listened intently to the stories of her famous father-in-law, and although she could not write, she managed to recall his stories and their experiences in great detail. In 1851, when Olive was almost seventy years old, she told many stories to Lyman C. Draper, who wanted to write a book chronicling the life of Daniel Boone.

Although we know little about Olive's youth, it is certain that like other girls growing up on the frontier, she learned the skills necessary to survive from her mother and other women in the family. At a young age, she probably learned to weave, sew, cook, tend livestock, harvest and preserve food, and treat common sicknesses and injuries. And, like other children, she probably grew up with stories of the wild frontier and of the dangers that were common.

Life for pioneer women was unpredictable and often dangerous. Indian attacks, disease, harsh weather, and a lack of familiarity with the land made the frontier a place where only a hardy few could survive. Frightening stories were told and retold, passed down in the community to serve as warnings.

Olive told Lyman Draper about an experienced frontiersman who disappeared in 1770 while on a hunting expedition with Daniel Boone. "I distinctly remember that Colonel Daniel Boone and Stewart had only separated to hunt or trap for some designated period and were then to meet at camp." While they were hunting, the Kentucky River flooded, trapping the two men on opposite sides. It wasn't until 1775, when building the Wilderness Road to the western territory, that they found Stewart's skeleton. Nearby was his powder horn, inscribed with his name.

Relationships between neighboring families often made the difference between success and failure. Death itself brought families together. Women frequently did not survive their childbearing years and men died young from accidents and battles. With no orphanages, neighboring families turned to one another to raise the surviving children. In just one generation, a complex web of relationships could bind families together; this was the case with the Boone and Vanbibber families.

Olive's family were known as "westering folk." Her father, Peter Vanbibber, had come to Botetourt County, Virginia, from Holland with his brother Isaac sometime before the American Revolution. In Botetourt, he met and married Marguery Bounds, and together they had ten children: Olive, the youngest, had six brothers and three sisters.

The alliance between the Vanbibbers and Boones may have first developed in 1774 when Isaac Vanbibber led a Virginia army that included Daniel Boone. In a battle at the junction of the Ohio and Kanawha Rivers, later known as Point Pleasant, eleven hundred frontiersmen fought a similar number of Native Americans and managed to defeat them, effectively eliminating them from the region. The frontiersmen made a small settlement there, in what was then Virginia. After division of the state in 1863, it became part of West Virginia.

Isaac Vanbibber died in the battle of Point Pleasant, leaving behind a widow and four children: John, Peter, Isaac, and Rebecca. John and Peter each found wives and settled in Powell's Valley, East Tennessee. It is unclear what happened to Isaac's widow and Rebecca; they may have gone to live with John or Peter.

According to Hazel Atterbery Spraker's *The Boone Family: A Genealogical History* (Baltimore: Genealogical Publishing Company, 1999), the remaining orphan, young Isaac, was adopted by Daniel and Rebecca Boone and raised as their own. It was not the first orphan child raised by the Boones. Two months before his wedding to Rebecca in 1756, Daniel took in the two sons of his deceased brother Israel. So, in marrying Daniel Boone, seventeen-year-old Rebecca instantly became the mother of two sons.

Daniel and Rebecca's son Nathan, Olive Vanbibber's future husband, was born on March 3, 1780, at Boone's Station, Kentucky. Daniel had established Boone's Station, now called Cross Plains, six miles northwest of Fort Boonesborough, a fort that protected settlers going west on the Wilderness Road through the Cumberland Gap.

Between 1775 and 1790, the non–Native American population of Kentucky, then part of the Commonwealth of Virginia, exploded from an estimated 150 to 73,000. By 1776, enough people lived there to make the General Assembly of Virginia designate Kentucky as a county. Three months before Nathan's birth, the general assembly divided Kentucky into three large counties and appointed Daniel Boone sheriff of Fayette County. He had been elected to the legislature and was on his way to meet with the legislature in Richmond, Virginia, when Nathan was born.

Rebecca was forty years old. Daniel was forty-five. They had been married for twenty years. The family lived in a large cabin with their sons Israel, Daniel Morgan, and Jesse Bryan, and daughters Levina and Rebecca. They were also raising the six children of Rebecca's uncle, James Bryan, whose wife had died.

A few years later, perhaps to enjoy a rest from the rigors of the wilderness, the Boones moved to the settlement at Point Pleasant where Daniel opened a store selling skins, furs, and other goods. Olive's family also lived in Point Pleasant, and Jesse Bryan Boone soon married her cousin, Chloe Vanbibber. Olive told Lyman Draper, "I am certain that my folks and Colonel Daniel Boone's family went to Point Pleasant when I was five years old and Nathan Boone was seven years old and so this would make it in 1787." The historian John Mack Faragher puts the Boones' move in 1789, however.

Using either date, the move came within a year of a 1788 experience that brought the Boone and Vanbibber families more closely together. According to John Mack Faragher, Daniel, Rebecca, and their sons, including seven-year-old Nathan, were transporting a keelboat full of ginseng root on the Ohio River to Hagerstown, Maryland, from where it would be shipped to China. As they neared Point Pleasant, the river's current became much stronger, and the boat hit a large log. It veered, then filled with water. Luckily, no one was hurt, but the ginseng was nearly destroyed.

The Boones were cold, wet, and exhausted when they arrived at the nearby home of John Vanbibber, Olive's cousin. According to Faragher, Daniel Boone had once rescued John Vanbibber in a snowstorm, and John was pleased to provide the Boone family with shelter and hospitality for several days while they rested and prepared to complete the journey to Hagerstown.

Although Daniel Boone's family sometimes traveled with him, more often, on the frontier, while a man was hunting, surveying, and scouting Indians, his wife was left at home with the children and slaves, if the family possessed them, for months or years. Highway robbers and vagrants took advantage of the isolation that left women and children vulnerable to the frontier's criminal element. Women had to survive as best they could in these unforgiving conditions to care for the children and maintain and protect the property their husbands had secured.

Olive was no doubt aware of the dangers from a young age. In 1789, when Olive was six, her niece and nephew, Rachel and Joseph Vanbibber, were attacked by Shawnee Indians as they crossed a river near a sugar maple grove where their father John was working. Rachel was killed and scalped on the spot, and Joseph was held captive. That same year Olive's aunt Brigetta was taken from her cabin by Indians and held captive. She eventually escaped or was released, but her husband and children had been killed when the cabin was attacked. Joseph and Jacob Vanbibber, who had been kidnapped in another incident, also returned, having either escaped or been redeemed, according to Faragher.

Settlements like Point Pleasant were often vulnerable to attacks from Indians desperately trying to protect their way of life. Occasionally, however, settlers and Indians helped each other.

Olive told Lyman Draper about one instance when her father-in-law extended his hand in kindness while he was waiting for his brother to return from a supply trip to North Carolina: "I have heard that when Daniel was waiting for Squire . . . he met an aged Indian who had been left to die by his tribe. He then killed a deer and keeping only a small quantity, gave the rest to the old Indian."

Daniel Boone moved his family from one patch of wilderness to another. The population of Kentucky kept growing; by 1792, it had enough citizens to become a state. Boone reacted by saying Kentuckians "were got too proud," and Nathan remembered that Daniel "said that when he left Kentucky, he did it with the intention of never stepping his feet upon Kentucky soil again; and if he was compelled to lose his head on the block or revisit Kentucky, he would not hesitate to choose the former."

After establishing himself as a merchant at Point Pleasant, Daniel moved the family in 1792 to a wilderness cabin sixty miles farther up Kanawha River, near present-day Charleston, West Virginia. Nathan stayed with his sister in Kentucky so he could attend a Baptist school.

When he returned from school, Nathan spent a few months in the wilderness with Daniel, then persuaded his father to move back to Kentucky—despite his earlier resolve never to return there—and build a log house at Brushy Creek.

When Olive's father died on October 10, 1796, Olive and her mother moved from Point Pleasant to the home of one of Olive's uncles in Ohio on the Ohio River. Two years later, Nathan moved to a cabin just twenty miles away. Daniel and Rebecca moved with him. Nathan and Olive now lived only a day's journey from each other.

The Boone and Vanbibber families had maintained the close connections established through adoption and early friendship. The Boone and Vanbibber men hunted together, offered each other assistance, and the families had been bound more closely through the marriage of Olive's cousin Chloe Vanbibber and Nathan's brother Jesse Bryan Boone.

In 1797, Daniel Morgan Boone, Nathan's older brother, headed to the Louisiana Territory to hunt and explore. The territory was under Spanish control, so Daniel Boone instructed his son to meet with the Spanish officials. Draper recorded Nathan's recollection: "He wanted to know the quantity of land granted to settlers, heads of families and children, and servants. He also wanted to know if settlers were required to embrace the Catholic religion."

The lieutenant governor of the Louisiana Territory, Zenon Trudeau, invited Daniel Morgan Boone to move to the territory. The Spanish government had heard that Daniel Boone made Kentucky a safe place for settlers and hoped he would do the same for Upper Louisiana. Trudeau wrote Daniel Boone a letter, Nathan Boone remembered. "He said that if he came, he should have 1,000 arpents of land for himself and that each family who came with him should be entitled to 600 arpents or perhaps 400 for the man, 40 arpents extra for his wife, and 40 arpents extra for each child and servant." An arpent is about eight-tenths of an acre. Daniel Morgan Boone told his friends and family that the area was beautiful and fertile, the perfect place for the Boone family to relocate.

By the time the family left for the Louisiana Territory in 1799, Nathan had fallen in love with Olive, who was known as "the handsomest woman north of the Ohio River." The two spent much time together and she was probably distraught at the thought of his leaving. He promised to write, and he asked that she take good care of herself in his absence.

Nathan, his brother Daniel Morgan, their sisters Susanna and Jemima, and Isaac Vanbibber's family traveled together, heading west on the Ohio River in mid-September 1799. Some of the party probably walked on the riverbank, watching for game they could shoot. Others may have ridden in the pirogue that Nathan and Daniel carved from a giant poplar tree. Nathan remembered: "This boat was five feet in diameter and between fifty and sixty feet long. It would hold five tons of our goods and family merchandise. We spent much time completing the boat, and it was not until fall that we were ready to start."

They planned to travel from the Ohio River to the Mississippi and Missouri to find the settlement Daniel Morgan had claimed. After only a few days, Nathan's traveling companions noticed that he was withdrawn and sad, not like himself. One of them asked what the trouble was. He answered that he was deeply in love with Olive and that, although he wanted to move with them, he could not overcome his feelings. The crew had traveled seventy-five miles, but after much deliberation, Nathan turned back. He would convince Olive to marry him, he resolved, and bring her west to join his family. Perhaps to seal his fate, he purchased a marriage license on the way.

Olive must have been surprised and pleased to see Nathan when he knocked on her cabin door. They married shortly after his arrival and began preparing for the journey west. The trip from Kentucky to the Louisiana Territory would be a grueling one, she knew, and would require exceptional stamina and courage. She also knew that life in the wild territory would be considerably tougher than it was in settled Kentucky.

Olive and Nathan were fortunate to have youth on their side. When they left, two months after their marriage, she was sixteen and he was eighteen. Aside from exuberance of spirit, they possessed little. Nathan spoke to Draper of his father's sentiments: "When I was married, it grieved the old colonel that he had nothing to give me and my wife with which to start our new life. He lamented his losses and misfortunes, but we thought none the less of him. He was rigidly honest and possessed nice perceptions of justice."

For their journey, Nathan and Olive each had a horse to ride and a pack horse. The pack horse carried some parched corn for food, an axe for cutting firewood, a few blankets, and probably a hunting knife. Nathan carried his rifle. The young couple survived on the parched corn, which Olive prepared, and the game Nathan was able to hunt. At night, they slept by an open fire. They rode through Lexington, Kentucky, and at Louisville they were joined by another couple, who traveled with them until they reached Vincennes. One of Olive and Nathan's horses had become lame, so they stayed in Vincennes for a few weeks while it healed. They met settlers and travelers and heard many stories about the west.

Years later, Olive reminisced, "We traveled along the rest of the way, arriving in St. Louis on the last of October. My husband was offered eighty acres of land west of the river for one of our ponies. He laughed and said he wouldn't give one of our ponies for the whole town." Olive went on to explain that Nathan knew that where they were going the pony would be worth much more. It is ironic that the eighty acres they were offered are now within the heart of St. Louis!

In preparation for crossing the Missouri at St. Charles, Nathan obtained a skiff and they loaded their possessions onto it. They led the three horses into the water. Olive sat in the stern as Nathan pushed the boat into the water. He handed her the horses' reins and jumped into the boat to row. Olive guided the craft to the opposite shore, holding the horses' reins as they swam alongside. When they reached the other side, Olive and Nathan were exhausted. They rested on the west bank of the river for a short while, allowing the horses to recuperate and drink from the river. Then they reloaded their supplies and were on their way. From there, the couple led the horses to a trail beside the river, which they followed until they reached the mouth of the Femme Osage, where the Boone family awaited.

Nathan soon found a job surveying roads for the Spanish government. Upon arriving in St. Louis in February, his father had received land concessions that corresponded with the number of people he brought with him. Because Nathan and Olive were not present, a space was not secured for them. Instead, they had to purchase property from Robert Hall, who had moved west with the Boones. They paid Hall with a horse, a saddle, and a bridle, together valued at $120.

And so, in January 1800, the young couple were the proud owners of 680 acres on the Femme Osage in the Louisiana Territory. Their land was situated about six or seven miles above the mouth of the Missouri River, in present-day St. Charles County. However, it was the height of winter and they would have to wait for spring before setting up a homestead. Daniel Morgan Boone invited them to live with him until the winter was over. Daniel and Rebecca Boone were also staying with him.

Daniel Morgan had made his home, a double cabin, on a bluff about a mile back from the mouth of the Missouri River, above St. Charles village. He had left his black slaves there to clear and cultivate his land while he traveled back to Kentucky to report to the rest of the family about the new territory. Nathan Boone later recalled for Lyman Draper that the slaves had "raised some ten or fifteen acres of crops, and so we were comfortably provided for that winter."

When the weather was warm enough, Nathan picked out a site and started building the first of many cabins he and Olive would occupy during their lives. He must have been anxious to hunt and explore with his father and brothers, or perhaps he was simply not prepared for the force and frequency of Missouri spring rainstorms. He failed to lay any materials to make a floor, leaving the ground bare, and did not construct a chimney. He laid shingles on top of the small cabin, but they did not protect the house from the water and wind.

Even though the cabin was barely finished, the call of the wilderness was far too enticing for young Nathan. He was off with his brother and father for his first Missouri hunt. He would be gone for months, leaving sixteen-year-old Olive, pregnant

A pioneer homestead was an industrious place where the family created almost everything they needed. This artist imagined a homestead with all the family in attendance, but in reality the men were often away, leaving women alone. (State Historical Society of Missouri, Columbia.)

with her first child, behind in the cabin with a slave woman approximately her own age.

Such an abrupt and sustained absence was not unusual at that time. It was typical for men to leave their families on the homestead for months. Once, when Rebecca and Daniel Boone were living in Kentucky, she did not see him for two years. When he returned, she presented him with a daughter, Jemima, born in his absence.

Even though it was common for women to be left alone, it was not easy for them. Just surviving day to day was difficult. While the men were away, women were in charge of protecting and improving the homestead. They cared for the livestock, planted and tended the crops, and fixed anything in need of repair. When Olive wanted fuel, she chopped wood. If she needed water, she hauled it.

After Nathan left on his hunting trip, rains turned the cabin's dirt floor to mud, and the water sometimes stood several inches deep. Olive and her young slave quickly set about improving the home themselves. Nathan remembered years later, "My dear wife, Olive, and her negro girl got poles to lay down, then peeled elm bark and laid it down as a floor, the rough side up to prevent its warping or rolling up." And so, when her husband returned from his hunt, he found that his young wife had constructed a cabin floor.

Nathan told another story about Olive's fine workmanship. Daniel Boone had built a shop for his tools, but he had cleared it out for Olive to put her loom there while the men were away hunting. Olive and her slave borrowed a crosscut saw from neighbors, which they used to "cut through several courses of logs until a suitable-sized aperture for a fireplace was made. Then with stones for the fireplace, sticks for the chimney, and mud for mortar, these lone women erected a chimney, the draft of which proved decidedly the best of any on the farm."

Making mortar, a thick paste of clay powder and water needed for the stonework, was heavy, time-consuming labor. The women had to dig up clay, dry it in the sun, break it to a powder, and sift out the rocks. However, they had no way to sift rocks from the clay, so Olive cut a piece of wood from a hickory tree and bent it together into a hoop. Overlapping the ends, she tied them together with bark strings. Then she killed a deer and treated the skin with ashes to preserve it. She stretched the skin tight over the hoop she had made, then heated a wire and used it to burn several holes in the animal hide. With this sieve, the two women were able to sift stones from clay to make the mortar they needed for the chimney.

Nathan remarked of his arrival at the homestead, "Upon our

return, we could scarcely believe the story of these architects." Not only had they made many improvements to the buildings, but the two young women had also finished the spring planting.

Immediately after returning to the Femme Osage, Nathan started construction on a larger and sturdier cabin. This new and improved home came just in time. Olive gave birth to her first child in July. They named this child James, for a brother Nathan had never known, killed by Indians who wanted to hold settlers east of the Appalachian Mountains in 1773. In her lifetime, Olive had fourteen children, one of whom died at birth. Such a large number of children born to one woman was not uncommon at the time.

Nathan supported Olive and their baby in a number of ways. Along with surveying, he spent considerable time laying traps and collecting skins to sell. In 1802, he left Olive to go trapping with his friend William T. Lamme. Together, the men ran a trap line all winter and caught nine hundred beavers, selling the skins for $2.50 each. Nathan reported that many of their best skins were stolen by Indians, however.

In 1804, their fourth year on the Femme Osage, Nathan and Olive moved into a log cabin about a half mile from Daniel Morgan Boone's house. Robert Hall had built the cabin but had left it after a short time. Nathan stopped hunting and began to cultivate the land around the cabin. Later that year, Daniel and Rebecca Boone moved from Daniel Morgan Boone's property to stay with Nathan and Olive. They built a "half-faced" camp, consisting of a cabin with three walls and open to the south to catch the sun, a cabin like those used for winter hunting camps when the Boones lived in Kentucky.

Daniel and Rebecca lived in their cabin in Nathan and Olive's backyard for many years. During that period, Olive grew close to Nathan's parents. From Daniel, she learned many stories of the frontier. From Rebecca, she learned much about surviving as a woman in the wilderness. Rebecca was known for her resource-fulness and perseverance, and also for her patient demeanor.

Much later, in an interview with Lyman Draper, Olive told a story that illustrated Rebecca's patience. On Rebecca's second meeting with Daniel, she said, "They sat upon a ridge of green turf under the cherry trees, and Daniel Boone was beside Rebecca Bryan and doubtless turning over in his own mind whether she would make him a good companion. At that time he took his knife out and, taking up one corner of her white apron, began to cut and stab holes through it, to which she said nothing nor offered any resistance." It was a story Daniel often told, and Olive explained that Daniel Boone had pulled this stunt in order to "try her temper, thinking if it was fiery, she would fly into a passion." Because she remained calm, Daniel declared, he decided to marry her.

Destroying a piece of fabric would have made some women furious. Women had to make use of every resource that came their way. Every thread had to be spun by hand and woven or knitted into useful things. Olive told Draper, "We used to gather nettles, a sort of hemp, toward spring, and when it became rotted by the wet weather, we could spin them. It was very strong. It grows in rich land about four feet high." A softer yarn was spun from buffalo wool and knitted into socks, "It was quite soft and wears very well."

Olive also learned the habits of the wild animals around her, their feeding habits, and when they were good for food. She told Draper:

> We found turkeys were very thin in summer because of ticks and made poor food. In the fall they would fatten rapidly on beech and other small mast. They were good eating in fall, winter, and spring. Buffaloes are best when eaten in the fall, as they feed upon grass, buffalo clover, and pea vine and feed

upon some acorns, chestnuts, and beechnuts. . . . The deer are also fattest in the fall. They live upon the same kind of food as buffalo, and the elk the same. About Christmas they would begin to thin down. They became very poor in the latter part of winter and early spring but in May began to improve. Frontier people probably found no wild bees and honey, as bees do not generally precede white settlements. There were none in the woods of Missouri until after the settlements expanded.

Like Rebecca, Olive lived most of her married life with the possibility that Nathan would not return, that he would die in the wilderness, killed by an Indian or wild animal. From time to time, the likelihood was brutally confirmed. In December 1804, Nathan went hunting and trapping with Olive's brother Mathias "Tice" Vanbibber. They had collected fifty-six beaver pelts and twelve otters and were near the Kansas River when they remembered that their wives had asked them to be home for the Christmas holiday.

As they headed back to the Boone camp, Nathan and Tice encountered twenty-two Osage Indians. Nathan recounted the tale to Lyman Draper, "They took our three horses and what furs we had and told us we had better clear out, for there was another party hunting for us." Nathan and Tice realized that the Osages had been honest with them when they heard another group of Indians coming. Luckily, they had time to hide. The next morning, they were met with still another party of Indians. "We ordered them off at gunpoint, but they said they were Sauks so were permitted to come in and eat . . . a compromise was reached, and we finally started off in company with those Indians. Soon other Indians joined them." Nathan was struck in the head by a ramrod, and a standoff developed. "Finally, the Indians said that if we would give them powder, balls, and flints, they might go." And so Nathan and Tice were left with one hunting rifle and five bullets. They had no coats or blankets and it was the middle of winter.

The two men used their first four bullets but killed nothing. Finally, Nathan was able to shoot a large panther. Nathan remembered, "This animal had a sweet and cattish taste. I cut the skin into two pieces and we each made a vest, cutting holes for inserting our arms and wearing the fur side next to our bodies." Eventually, they found the trail that led to a camp of American frontiersmen, including Nathan's nephew, James Callaway. The men brought them home, both on the brink of death from extreme shock. Olive remarked many years later, "It was the first Christmas he had spent at home since our marriage, and I had the Indians to thank for that." Tice did not recover from this incident; he held on for two years, mostly confined to his bed, until his death.

In 1805, Nathan went to the Great Osage village on Pomme de Terre Creek to recover the horses and traps that had been stolen from him on his hunting expedition with Tice. A trader told him that the robbery had been committed by members of the Little Osage nation. But when Nathan went to the Little Osage settlement he couldn't find the culprits. The Great Osage Chief White Hair had sent several of his braves to help Nathan find the horses. But when the braves arrived, the horses had been hidden away, and only the traps could be recovered.

In 1806, Nathan, Daniel Morgan Boone, and three other men established the Boone's Lick Salt Manufactory twelve miles northwest of the present town of Boonville in Howard County, Missouri. In the beginning, Nathan and his partners shipped twenty-five to thirty bushels of salt per day by dugout canoe to settlements on the river. Salt was essential for preserving meat, animal skins, and produce, which made it of great value to early settlers.

In the first year, the salt manufactory had six to eight men working, then a few years later, sixteen to twenty men, producing a hundred bushels a day. Eventually, Nathan, his brothers, and their fellow investors quit the business for lack of profits. The Missouri Department of Natural Resources purchased and now maintains a fifty-acre historic site where the lick once was. Visitors to the Boone's Lick Historic Site may follow a trail that leads down the wooded hillside to the salt springs.

In March 1812, preparing to declare war on Great Britain, President James Madison appointed Nathan as a captain of the Missouri Rangers, which became widely known by the less official names "Boone's Mounted Rangers" and "The Minutemen of the Frontier." The group of a hundred men were volunteers, and they paid for everything they needed to patrol the Missouri frontier, including weapons, horses, clothing, and food.

Olive knew that this position would put her husband in danger, and it is likely that she often heard stories of how he had narrowly escaped death. According to one famous tale she probably heard many times, the mounted rangers were on a particularly long campaign near present-day Peoria, Illinois. On the second day out, they camped along a shallow creek. Around midnight, one of Nathan's sentries reported that a group of Indians was attempting to surround the encampment. Nathan awakened and quietly helped his troops escape to the other side of the creek. When the Indians caught sight of Nathan's figure in the darkness, and were sure they had spotted Captain Boone himself, they carefully aimed their muskets. However, as luck would have it, Nathan just happened to step into a sinkhole and suddenly fall. The Indians fired, but Nathan hit the ground and thus survived to tell the story. By the time the mounted rangers returned home, there was snow on the ground, and they had completely worn out their boots. They had wrapped strips of animal hide around their feet to keep them from freezing.

Back home on the Femme Osage, Olive and her neighbors struggled through the days. Boone's rangers had built a network of forts and blockhouses where settlers could gather when there was danger of attack. According to the historian R. Douglas Hurt, the neighbors used the shelters to keep safe twice between 1812 and the end of the War of 1812–1814.

Mary Boone Hosman, Nathan and Olive's youngest daughter, spoke to many reporters and historians over the years. She remembered that her father was often away from home for months on end, so long that her mother would believe him dead. Then one day, with no notice, he would arrive home. "He would go into the bedroom, and take off a concealed canvas belt on which had been sewn two canvas pockets. These pockets would be full of gold, for the government paid its soldiers in gold."

In 1813, Rebecca Boone died. She had gone on a trip with her husband to visit their daughter Jemima's house in the early spring. Jemima and Flanders Callaway had a grove sugar maple trees located about a mile away from Olive and Nathan's house. Rebecca and Daniel greatly enjoyed traveling there for the annual sugar spinning time. One day, Rebecca complained that she was feeling ill. Daniel brought her in from the grove to Jemima's house to rest, but he could not save her. She died there at the age of seventy-four.

Daniel missed Rebecca greatly after her passing, and he gave up his home. He spent considerable time at the home of Jemima and Flanders, so that he could be close to Rebecca's resting place. He also stayed at the homes of his sons Daniel Morgan and Jesse Bryan Boone as well as with Nathan and Olive.

In their travels from St. Charles to their salt processing operation, Nathan and Daniel Morgan Boone had developed the route west to present-day Howard County that became known as the Booneslick Trail or Trace, followed by many early settlers after 1812. It later joined the Santa Fe Trail.

Sometime during 1816, five years before Missouri became a state, Nathan began construction of a permanent two-story stone house near the Femme Osage in Defiance, Missouri. He wanted it to look like the houses he had seen while visiting the

The stone home in Defiance where Daniel Boone died is a monument not only to the Boone family but also to the skills of its builders—itinerant workmen and slaves. A product of a dangerous time, its walls were two and a half feet thick and had gun ports for long rifles in the event of an attack. A few years after its completion, the house was shaken in the New Madrid Earthquake and dropped several inches as the earth shifted under it—yet the only damage was a hairline crack on a fireplace in the basement. (Photo by Margot Ford McMillen.)

Boone family homestead in Berks County, Pennsylvania, as an eight-year-old boy with his parents. Many know it as the home of Daniel Boone and incorrectly credit its construction to him. In truth, Nathan, Olive, and their children and slaves were the primary builders and occupants of the structure. The elegant stonework has led to speculation that experienced masons may also have been employed. The stone home is now maintained and operated as a historic site by Lindenwood University.

In the late summer of 1820, Daniel Boone died in Nathan's home. He was eighty-five years old. Of course, there are many stories of his last years and death. In *The History of Dade County and*

*Her People,* published in 1917, Howard Ragsdale recounts a story that "Aunt Mary" Hosman, Nathan's daughter, told of Colonel Boone's leaving Nathan and Olive's house without a word to anyone about where he was going or what he was doing. He took with him one of Nathan's young male slaves and returned months later in autumn, with stories of his journey up the Missouri River, across the state, to the mouth of the Kansas River. He described the entire trip, including his discovery of salt springs on his travels. He died soon thereafter and was buried beside Rebecca.

Another, more reliable version of Boone's last years is from the manuscripts of Lyman Draper. In this story, Daniel Boone made the trek to daughter Jemima's home to visit Rebecca's grave and see his daughter. Nathan told Draper: "He had an attack of the fever, not severe, and while recovering was exceedingly anxious to be taken to my house. My wife and I visited the old man and he insisted on going back with us." They postponed the trip for a few weeks, as the doctor warned Daniel that any more traveling could be the death of him. Nathan arrived at his sister's home with a carriage for Daniel and brought him back to the stone house on September 12. He was weak and exhausted, but he refused medical treatment. Nathan remembered, "He said it was his last sickness, but, he said calmly, he was not afraid to die."

Boone's family, friends, and neighbors were all there with him. Olive prepared a special meal, including his favorite, sweet potatoes. She put him to bed in a bedroom on the bottom floor of the stone house. Everyone gathered around and Olive sang some of his favorite songs as he requested. In the morning, he asked his relatives and slaves to come to his bedside and said goodbye. The date was September 26, 1820. As he had asked, his family buried him in a coffin carved of black walnut, which he had ordered for himself when Rebecca died. He was buried beside the resting place of his beloved wife.

In 1832, Nathan and Olive sold 288 acres in the Femme Osage bottom to William Cashon for $1,032. They had sacrificed most

of their land, at one time around 680 acres, in order to pay off
a loan that Nathan had cosigned for a county official who had
then defaulted on the loan and misappropriated public funds.
By 1833, Nathan and Olive had only a few acres and the stone
house to call their own.

In 1833, Nathan was ordered back into military service because of growing Indian hostilities and was reinstated as captain
of the Missouri Mounted Rangers to fight the Blackhawk War.
He became captain of the First Regiment of Dragoons and was
to serve in that capacity for twenty years. This return to the
military may have gained Nathan much fame, but it took him
over a hundred miles from Olive.

One evening, in 1833, Nathan camped in the forests of Greene
County. After settling in for the evening, the story goes, he took a
look around him and was struck by the beauty of the Ozark hills.
He was pleased that the area had apparently not been cultivated
or farmed. That night, Nathan decided that he and Olive would
move to this place, and that he would call it Ash Grove.

Nathan arrived at the stone house in late July. Olive and the
children, who hadn't seen him in several months, had again been
worried that he was dead. Although this was a common worry
for Olive, she tried hard to shield her children from the pain she
experienced during her husband's long absences. Mary Hosman
remembered that in those days her mother would often retire to
her room early and, when she thought her children were out of
earshot, cry herself to sleep.

Olive agreed to move to Ash Grove. A German visitor, Hein-
rich von Martels, had seen her at the stone house on the Femme
Osage in November 1833. His story, recently translated from
German by Adolf Schroeder, summarizes the stories about
Nathan told among the new German immigrants crowding into
St. Charles and Warren Counties in the 1830s and gives a rare
account of a meeting with Olive.

When Nathan returned after months or years in the military, he brought back gold coins as pay. Olive would hold her husband's upturned hat in her hands to catch the gold pieces as he counted and tossed them to her. (State Historical Society of Missouri, Columbia.)

A German told me that Major Boone had offered him his property located at Femme Osage . . . for $4,000. We went there but unfortunately the major, who commanded the volunteers (the Rangers) on the last War against the Indians, had gone to Arkansas and will not be back until next summer.

We offered Mrs. Boone $3,800 and a significant amount for corn, animals, and furniture, but she was not able to conclude the sale in the absence of her husband although she wished to very much.

The story of the experiences of this lady touched me deeply. Thirty years ago at age 16, with her . . . husband, she left Kentucky. They owned nothing but the horses which they rode, a rifle, an axe, and a few blankets.

So they came up the Mississippi and the Missouri to the beautiful valley of the Femme Osage. They both liked the place where their house now stands and where five strong springs flow from the ground. Both immediately shouted, "Here we want to build a cabin." Quickly they built a cabin from logs and the bark of cottonwood trees and the young couple lived from the spoils of the hunt, on which she always accompanied her husband. It was an easy thing for them to kill 6 to 7 deer and a few bears daily.

. . . Boone understood the art of surveying and through it and with the spoils of the hunt increased his fortune, and he was in a position to clear a sizable field and have a house built which cost $4000. A flourishing family of ten children surrounded them and his father, Old Colonel Boone, lived with him the last days of his noteworthy life.

But unfortunately this good fortune did not remain; troubles developed when Boone signed a security for someone he thought to be his friend. But the latter secretly sold his possessions and fled. Boone now had to take over the debt of $5000; although his creditors offered him very favorable terms, he does not want to accept them but wants to pay everything and to accomplish this, sell his estate and move to Arkansas. . . .

A great number of friends will follow Major Boone when he moves . . . next year, and this will give Germans an opportunity to buy beautiful farms at good prices.

In 1837, the Boones sold their property on the Femme Osage for $6,120. With their sons James, Benjamin Howard, and John Coburn, they arrived at Ash Grove during the spring of 1837.

Nathan Boone is generally credited with building the cabin in Ash Grove. However, archaeological and historical investigations conducted by Southwest Missouri State University for the Missouri Department of Natural Resources uncovered evidence

The Ash Grove home of Nathan and Olive Boone, now a State Historical Site, is constructed of walnut logs. A double cabin or "dog trot" style, each floor consists of two large rooms divided by a hallway. The wide wooden planks in the floor are held together by pegs carved from the same wood. Large chimneys on each end of the house seem to hold the house together. (State Historical Society of Missouri, Columbia.)

to the contrary. According to that research, Olive and her sons were the primary planners of the home. The Boones' slaves—the family collectively possessed at least twelve—provided most of the actual labor for the house's construction.

Archaeological investigations also uncovered other structures the Boones used, including a stone-lined storage cellar, smokehouse, summer kitchen, and front walkway. It also revealed the Boone family cemetery and an African American cemetery. The site of the slave quarters has never been found.

When Nathan died, he owned eleven slaves. In one interview, Robert L. Hosman, a great-grandson of Olive and Nathan, remembered his grandmother Mary Hosman telling about a large

The house has two spacious rooms upstairs for sleeping. The log rafters are exposed and easily seen. (Photo by Margot Ford McMillen.)

log home "a stone's throw away" from Nathan and Olive's cabin. This may have been the home where Nathan and Olive's slaves lived. They may have shared the house with the slaves of Benjamin Boone, who owned adjacent property. Three of the slaves may have stayed on the farm and taken the Boone name after Emancipation.

A tornado in 1937 destroyed much of the farming operation at Ash Grove. However, DNR researcher Jeffrey K. Yelton thinks that the Boones may have bred horses to sell. According to county tax records, Nathan owned 7 (male) horses, 9 mares, 3 colts, 4 fillies, and 1 stallion. The probate records indicate that Nathan and Olive grew wheat, corn, potatoes, and oats.

In 1851, Boone historian and friend Lyman Draper came from New York to visit Olive and Nathan at Ash Grove. He stayed with them for three weeks, interviewing them about the life of Daniel Boone, so that he could complete his book on the celebrated frontiersman. Draper was never able to write the book he planned, but his papers at the Wisconsin Historical Society have been of great value to historians.

Draper wanted to tell the real story of Daniel Boone, a large task when one considers that Daniel Boone had become a man of near mythological proportions. However, Nathan and Olive seemed to trust Draper's judgment, and they gave him a pack of original Boone family notes. Nathan testified for Draper that he considered Draper's work to be "prepared with so much care and faithfulness, . . . which alone will hand down to posterity any thing like a correct view of my father's public and private career."

Many of the family stories came to Draper from Olive, who had learned them from Daniel Boone. For example, Daniel had witnessed the gruesome death of an older son, Israel, in a 1782 battle with Indians at Blue Licks during the Revolutionary War. At the time of the event, Nathan was about a year and a half old. Olive told Draper: "Colonel Boone got the Widow Edward Boone's horse . . . and gave it to Israel to mount and ride off. Israel said, 'Father, I won't leave you,' and the colonel told him to make his escape, and he would find another horse. Colonel Boone went to get another, heard something, looked around . . . and saw him falling. The blood was gushing from his mouth several inches and his arms were stretched out and shivering. . . . They found Israel had been shot through the heart." Returning after the battle for the dead, the burial party found that most of the bodies had been scalped. Flocks of vultures had found the bodies, which had decomposed in the summer heat.

At the time of Draper's visit, Nathan considered himself to be in feeble health. Although he stayed at home, he kept his commission in the army until 1853, resigning at age seventy-two. By October 1856 he realized he would not live much longer, and on October 12 he dictated his will. Four days later, Nathan Boone died.

He left his "beloved wife, Olive Boone," all of their worldly possessions, including the house and farming operation, "during her lifetime." His youngest son, Benjamin Howard, who had lived with his parents, reported that "he said nothing about dying. . . . [H]e only spoke of wanting his will written so that he could provide for Mother."

Two sons-in-law protested the will, and Olive eventually renounced it, declaring her children as heirs. She agreed to sell most of the property, and on November 24, 1856, she held a sale. On the auction block were 74 hogs, 25 sheep, 23 horses, 8 oxen, 5,600 bushels of oats, 70 bushels of wheat, several hundred bushels of corn, furniture, farm equipment, and the eleven slaves. The sale of the slaves brought $9,006, and other items, including livestock and household goods, brought $3,928.75. Olive kept the log home and the property surrounding it and continued to live there until she died in 1858.

For years, the log cabin in Ash Grove, with a small family cemetery with the graves of Olive, Nathan, and other close relatives, went largely unrecognized.

Nathan and Olive's homestead stood unmarked until May 1942, when a memorial marker was placed on Nathan's grave by the Daughters of the American Revolution, recognizing his service in the United States Mounted Rangers. The cabin was occupied by several families, off and on, until the 1960s, when it was mostly forgotten.

In 1991, the Missouri Department of Natural Resources acquired the house and its 371-acre tract of land. Even though Olive stayed home and Nathan was away much of the time they

For years, no monument existed to memorialize the life of Olive Boone. The cemetery was unfenced and animals grazed through it. Participants in the Nathan Boone Rendezvous, first held in 1984, noticed there was no monument to Olive, and with the help of the DAR and Lawrence and Dorothy Strader of Ash Grove they acquired a headstone to match Nathan's, which was installed in 1942 by the DAR in recognition of his service in the War of 1812. A special supplement to the Commonwealth and Ash Grove *Shopping News* of September 16–17, 1992, reported that Olive's stone was installed in an "impressive ceremony" in September 1985. (Photo by Margot Ford McMillen.)

owned the property, the Department of Natural Resources calls the site the Nathan Boone State Historic Site. The DNR will use it to reflect the experience of pioneer Missourians who settled on the prairies of southwest Missouri.

The home today is protected by weatherboarding and metal siding, which will be removed when the restoration is completed. One stone chimney tumbled in the tornado of 1937; the other still stands intact. A black locust tree, which witnessed the last chapters of Olive's long life, still stands.

The story of Olive Boone's life stands as a testament to the bravery and perseverance of the many frontier women who left their settled towns and homes for wild, uncharted territories. Although the credit for taming the American West usually goes to explorers and hunters like Daniel and Nathan Boone, the constant labors of women like Olive Boone and other courageous women should be recognized as well.

## FOR MORE READING

*My Father, Daniel Boone: The Draper Interviews with Nathan Boone,* edited by Neal O. Hammon (Lexington: University Press of Kentucky, 1999), is the published edition of the 1851 interviews Lyman C. Draper conducted at Ash Grove with Nathan and Olive Boone. Although the primary focus is on the life of Daniel Boone, some delightful stories of Olive and Nathan Boone's lives are discussed. Olive's voice is nicely preserved through this work.

*Nathan Boone and the American Frontier,* by R. Douglas Hurt (Columbia: University of Missouri Press, 1998), discusses Olive's life briefly, as it concentrates primarily on the activities of her husband. However, it is a delightful read and effectively sets apart the accomplishments of Nathan Boone from those of his father.

In addition to providing a remarkably accessible, balanced portrait of the great man, *Daniel Boone: The Life and Legend of an American Pioneer,* by the award-winning historian John Mack Faragher (New York: Henry Holt, 1992), also includes generous information about the women connected to Daniel Boone's life, including his mother, Sara Morgan Boone; his wife, Rebecca Bryan Boone; Olive Boone; and Jemima Boone Callaway, his daughter. Faragher's colorful but accurate portrayal brings the pioneer family to life.

Carole Bills compiled a collection of the writings of Springfield columnist Lucile Morris Upton and local historian John K. Hulston in *Nathan Boone: The Neglected Hero* (Republic, Mo.: Western Printing, 1984). It has information on the Nathan Boone family, Nathan's will, the auction, and the Nathan Boone Homesite.

# 3

## *Martha Jane Chisley Tolton*

At the church, hundreds of people stood in line to come forward to ask for a blessing. Before laying his hands on the others, Father Augustine Tolton laid his hands on the head of his mother, invoking God's blessing on this woman whose Catholic faith governed every aspect of her life.

—Father Roy Bauer, *They Called Him Father Gus*

Learning about the life of any early nineteenth-century person is difficult. This is especially true for enslaved African American women. We know the story of Martha Jane Chisley Tolton, the mother of the first nationally known African American Catholic priest, only because of records left by her son and their friends.

Martha Jane Chisley was born in 1833 on the John Manning plantation in Mead County, Kentucky. Her parents, Augustine Chisley and Matilda Hurd, were slaves. In 1849, Martha Jane's owner gave her and five other slaves as a wedding present to his stepdaughter. The newlyweds, Stephen and Susan Elliott, took her with the other slaves to a farm in Ralls County, Missouri, about nineteen miles southwest of Hannibal. Sixteen-year-old Martha Jane Chisley would never see her family or childhood friends again.

Martha Jane remembered that her owner came to the slave

quarters with a bucket of red paint. When he nodded, the overseer dabbed a red spot on the forearm of certain slaves. They had no idea what it meant; later, they learned they were going to Ralls County as a gift for the newly married Elliotts.

Ralls County was mostly prairie at the time the Elliotts settled in the neighborhood of Brush Creek, near Monroe City, but the area would soon change. In 1847, developers had gained a charter to build a railroad westward from Hannibal to St. Joseph, Missouri, passing through Ralls County and giving farmers a way of sending their products to the Mississippi River for shipping to city markets.

Construction on the railroad did not begin until 1852, when Congress granted six hundred thousand acres to the developers. Well before that time, increasing numbers of settlers had begun moving into the area. Immigrants from Ireland, Germany, and England claimed farmland in the area, but they were far out-numbered by Kentuckians and other Southerners, continuing a migration that began much earlier, in the late 1790s, when the Daniel Boone family settled in Spanish Louisiana. So many Southerners came to Ralls County in the early 1800s that some historians include it as a part of Missouri's "Little Dixie" region, primarily across the central part of the state.

Among the Kentuckians settling in northeast Missouri were a number of Elliott men and their families, drawn by cheap land and the fact that slavery was legal. The Elliotts, like most others in their community, supported their church and made sure that their slaves practiced their religion. Like many slave owners, Protestant and Catholic, they felt a duty to save the souls of the enslaved blacks they used as labor. The Elliotts were Catholics, and back in Kentucky Martha Jane's owners had made sure she was baptized soon after birth. For both owner Susan Elliott and slave Martha Jane, Catholic religious practices, the stories of the Bible, and Christian beliefs gave meaning to their days of hard work.

The site of Father Tolton's childhood church in Missouri—St. Peter's Brush Creek—is now on the National Register of Historic Places. The log church where he was baptized was replaced in 1862 with a stone church built by an Irish stonemason. It is a remarkable example of vernacular architecture with its limestone and sandstone facade and large windows topped with pointed arches. (Photo by Adolf E. Schroeder.)

The typical farmer in the Little Dixie counties raised wheat, corn, rope hemp, and tobacco to sell on the national and international markets. As crops, hemp and tobacco were particularly labor-intensive. Hemp stalks grew in dense masses towering ten feet high. To harvest hemp with the hand scythes available at the time was strenuous work, and after the cut the workers had to scatter the stalks in the field to dry, then bundle them in enormous bales for shipping. By 1856, the McCormick Company had introduced a hemp reaper pulled by mules, making possible a quicker harvest. But hand labor was needed for other activities such as spreading out the stalks to dry in the field and making the dried hemp into bales.

Tobacco was a demanding crop because the plants had to be trimmed weekly in the growing season to produce good leaves. Then, the leaves were hung up in a special barn where they dried by air circulation or from the heat of a wood fire. When they had dried, or "cured," the leaves were bundled and shipped; tobacco culture was a year-round job.

Both slave women and men worked in the fields, but Martha Jane Chisley may have worked in the house under the supervision of Susan Elliott. House servants had some privileges. They sometimes had better food than field slaves and were better clothed. Martha Jane undoubtedly had a better opportunity to learn than the slaves who worked all day in the fields.

Still, work was unending. The women prepared meals, preserved food for winter, and sewed by hand most of the clothing. Clothes washing and mending were on the long list of "women's work." With no supermarkets or malls, the family meals came from the farm's hogs, chickens, milk cows, orchard, and gardens. Slave women provided such valuable help to white women that, when her black slave died, one white housewife from Boone County wrote, "[I]t almost broke me up for I have eight in the family and the only girl I have to help me is six years old."

Although Missouri had come into the Union in 1821 as a slave state, not all Missourians favored slavery. Many European immigrants had come to the New World to escape political oppression, and most did not believe in slavery. Many other settlers, including some from the South, were also opposed to slavery. Throughout the 1840s and 1850s, tensions between slaveholders and those opposed to slavery increased nationally and in Missouri, which was surrounded on three sides by free states or territories—the states of Illinois and Iowa, and the territory of Kansas. Abolitionists frequently came through Missouri, telling slaves about the "Underground Railroad" and helping those who wanted to escape.

The Underground Railroad, a covert network of abolitionists

organized to help slaves to freedom, adopted the language of other railroads as a kind of code. "Conductors" helped slaves along the "line," sometimes transporting the "freight" in wagons. "Stations" or "depots" were about twenty miles apart, the distance a man could comfortably walk in one day.

Located across the Mississippi River from Missouri, Quincy, Illinois, was one of three major Illinois starting points for the Underground Railroad that led to the "terminus" at Chicago. As early as 1824, some Quincy abolitionists petitioned the state to change the constitution and recognize slaves as free people once they entered the state. Yet the town's proslavery Southerners lived side by side with Northerners, and all wished to live peacefully, as their businesses depended on products from both sides of the river and on free traffic between the states.

In 1836, David Nelson, a Southern doctor, had renounced slavery and moved with his family to Missouri, where he became the president of Marion College in Philadelphia, near Palmyra. Finding his views extremely unpopular in Missouri, he moved to Quincy to start again. Nelson's Mission Institute became a self-supporting school built by students, both male and female. The classical education provided by Mission Institute included Greek, mathematics, and astronomy, but the school was also known as an abolitionist training school.

On July 24, 1841, three men from Quincy rowed across the Mississippi River to Missouri and stopped at several farms to persuade slaves to flee to freedom. One slave owner heard the men talking to the slaves, urging them to go along with the plan. When the abolitionists were captured, he testified to what he had heard. The men were found guilty and sentenced according to the law of the time—twelve years in the Missouri State Penitentiary. This attempt to "steal" slaves was widely publicized in the area and caused continuing tension.

Slave owners, dependent on slaves for labor, considered the abolitionists a serious threat to their livelihood. When a slave

Slaves were considered property and could be bought or sold at the slave-owner's pleasure. Husbands and wives, parents and children could be separated forever. The fear of being "sold South" kept many slaves from trying to escape. (State Historical Society of Missouri, Columbia.)

disappeared from home, the owner advertised in newspapers, offering rewards for his or her return. Slave owners patrolled the roads, looking for runaways, and they often sold recaptured slaves to traders from the South, a fate slaves in Missouri greatly feared.

In 1847, Missouri legislators passed laws intended to prevent slave rebellion. These laws prevented blacks from meeting without white supervision. Additionally, anyone who taught a slave to read or write could be fined or put in jail, and free blacks or mulattoes were prohibited from moving into the state. These laws were aimed at keeping slaves on their owners' farms. Still, even while living on isolated farms, slaves saw each other at church, or in the fields. They shared stories about free blacks they heard about. Martha Jane Chisley must have heard about the free state across the river.

The Elliotts lived near another Catholic family, the James Hagars. Like the Elliotts, the Hagars had come with slaves and a full set of relatives—brothers, uncles, cousins. Among the Hagar slaves was Peter Paul Tolton, who had been baptized at St. Peter's Brush Creek Church, a small log church built in 1846. Peter Paul Tolton was named for Peter Paul LeFevre, the visiting priest who baptized him. St. Peter's Brush Creek Church was a mission of St. Paul's at the time and did not have enough members to support a full-time pastor. According to family tradition, Tolton and Martha Jane Chisley met when she called for him to help a slave boy who had collapsed. He was moved by her tenderness in helping the boy.

We have no pictures of Peter Paul or Martha Jane. From photos of their son Augustine and one photo of their daughter, Anne, we know their children were tall, strong-looking, and handsome.

Even though slave marriage was forbidden in Missouri, the Elliotts made sure that Martha Jane and Peter Paul were married by a priest at St. Peter's Brush Creek Church. The Hagars agreed that the couple could live on the Elliott farm, although Peter

This image of Martha Jane's daughter, Anne, is a rare photo of a nineteenth-century African American woman. It was made in Quincy, perhaps at the time of her brother's return to the community. We might imagine that her mother was equally strong and beautiful. (Tolton Collection, University Archives, Brenner Library, Quincy University.)

continued to work for the Hagars. When they had children, the children belonged to the Elliotts.

The Toltons had three children. The eldest was a son whom they named Charles, after one of Martha Jane's brothers and the priest who had baptized him, Rev. Charles J. Coomes, who was also her brother's godfather. Father Coomes served their Kentucky parish at least until 1875 and remembered Martha Jane and her brother, even writing to her after the Civil War. There is no doubt that he was the first of many priests who nourished Martha Jane's love for the Church.

On April 1, 1854, when their second son was born, they named him Augustine John. Augustine said later that his name was given for Martha Jane's father, Augustine Chisley, and for St. Augustine, the great African theologian. John was the patron saint of Father John O'Sullivan, who baptized Augustine at Brush Creek Church. His baptismal record states: "a colored child born April 1, 1854, son of Peter Tolton and Martha Chisley, property of Stephen Elliott." Susan Elliott was named as the baby's godmother.

A Ralls County census taken in 1860 shows four Elliott families with heads of households named "Stephen," all from Kentucky. The Stephen E. Elliott family includes his wife, "Ann S. Elliott." This must be "Susan." By 1860, the couple would have been married eleven years. The census reports seven Elliott children.

A John and Sarah are fourteen years old, perhaps the children of an earlier marriage or those of another family. There are five other Elliott children: Francis, eleven; William, eight; Alice, five; Angelican, three; and James, two. The Tolton family is included as part of the Stephen E. Elliott household in the 1860 slave census. The Tolton children were Charles, age eight; Augustine, six; and Anne, only a few months old. A nine-year-old mulatto girl is also listed in the household.

During the decade before the Civil War, Ralls County was

growing and prospering. In 1852, a plank road was built for the stagecoach from Hannibal to Paris. It passed the Elliott and Hagar farms. The railroad, which passed about five miles from the farms, was completed from Hannibal to Monroe City in 1857, and to St. Joseph in 1859. With the railroad, products from eastern factories became available, and life got a little easier.

There was still plenty of work, but Martha Jane found time to pass the traditions of singing and praying to the children from their earliest days. Augustine said later that he learned to pray and sing "at his mother's knee." The church stories and hymns had a special meaning for the slaves. When the slaves sang about Moses leading the enslaved children of Israel to freedom, they thought about their own condition and longed to be free.

April 13, 1861, when secessionists fired on Fort Sumpter, South Carolina, is the date historians consider the official starting date for the Civil War. Secession groups, wanting to break away from the Union, quickly formed in the Southern states. Although some officials tried to keep the state neutral, Missouri was almost immediately torn between the disputing sides. Many citizens professed their allegiance to one side or the other. Secessionist "State Guard" units formed in many parts of the state, while Union sympathizers also organized in large numbers.

The situation offered an opportunity for extremists and outlaws to take advantage of the confusion. Throughout the Civil War in Missouri, groups claiming to be on one side or the other burned entire towns and farms to the ground and plundered food stores, leaving people to go hungry.

In Ralls County, the battles started soon after war was declared. Union leaders in St. Louis wanted to ensure control of the Hannibal–St. Joseph Railroad. In July 1861, landowners who wanted to keep control of the railroad formed a State Guard near Florida, Missouri. James Hagar, the owner of Peter Paul Tolton, was among those who established the Guard, but Stephen Elliott's name is not included on the roll.

The State Guard, mostly slaveholders, pledged to protect the railroad and the county against the Union troops. They did not have to wait long for a challenge. On July 8, 1861, Union soldiers arrived in Monroe City from Palmyra, a town on the railroad line where they had camped. They brought not only men but also a cannon, a piece of equipment that would surely overwhelm the farmers of the State Guard, who carried only hunting rifles and pistols.

The Federal men, with their cannon, began their slow march to Florida for northeast Missouri's first battle of the Civil War. In a skirmish on a hill called "Hagar's Hill," owned by Robert Hagar, the Federal troops suffered a loss of at least one man and a half-dozen horses. They camped there, staying two nights. An eyewitness wrote that "Many families through fear had left their homes. All such were robbed of everything that they could carry off, furniture broken up, etc. . . . Henneries and pigstys were robbed. Both Union and Secessionists have suffered very much."

The Federal troops then marched back to Monroe City and found that the railroad station and several railroad cars had been destroyed. They took over a two-story brick building and sent for reinforcements.

Now the State Guard saw an opportunity. The chance to humiliate Federal soldiers was almost as agreeable as a victory would have been. As the secessionists surrounded the brick building, spectators came from miles around to see the excitement and to hear the speeches of the leaders. Women and children came in carriages, prepared for a picnic.

The holiday mood was broken when Union reinforcements came to the aid of their men trapped in the building. Nobody was hurt, but most of the secessionists located their wives or neighbors and galloped back home. As one described later, "The prairie was covered with buggies, carriages, wagons, horsemen and footmen—all fleeing for dear life." The picnic was over. The countryside had been devastated, and it was too late to replant or to raise new animals for winter meat.

In the chaos after the skirmish, the relationship between slave and master in Ralls County was transformed. We do not know the exact circumstances of the Elliott and Hagar farms after the battle, but we know that around this time Peter Paul Tolton disappeared to join the Union army.

In St. Louis, on August 30, 1861, Federal general Charles Fremont extended martial law, which had been ordered in St. Louis, to the entire state and declared that Missourians who had taken up arms against the Union would forfeit all property, including slaves, who could go free. National policy promised freedom only to the slaves whose owners would force them to fight against the Union, and when he learned of Fremont's action President Abraham Lincoln urged him to bring his command in line with national policy. When Fremont refused, President Lincoln himself rescinded the orders, allowing Missouri slave owners to keep their slaves as long as they did not force them to fight against the Union troops.

In the confusion, Martha Jane Tolton left the Elliott farm with her children, hoping to cross the Mississippi River to freedom and make her way to the community of free blacks in Quincy, Illinois. It was a desperate act, but sometimes a woman has to have the courage to take a brave leap and trust she will land on her feet. For Martha Jane, there were to be many brave leaps, and her confidence was rewarded. In 1861, she got her children into free Illinois.

Father Landry Genosky wrote that Mrs. Tolton probably followed the plank road, walking twenty miles to Hannibal. One story holds that a white neighbor helped them. Tolton family history records that Union soldiers helped Martha Jane find a rowboat in Hannibal and that Confederate soldiers fired on the boat as the family crossed the wide river. Speaking in 1928 in

Philadelphia, Augustine said that a reward of two hundred dollars was offered for them, "dead or alive." The family arrived safely in Illinois, and workmen gave them food and helped them on their way.

After reaching Illinois, the family walked another twenty miles —another day—to Quincy. Since it was the second-largest city in Illinois after Chicago, Martha Jane could have seen Quincy's buildings a long way off—huge and perhaps intimidating. Was she excited? Did the family sing as they approached the city? Were they simply too hungry and exhausted to feel anything? It is impossible to tell. But Martha Jane had accomplished her goal. They were in a free state where people would help them, and there were Catholic churches to attend.

There are at least two stories, each with many variations, about the Toltons' journey from Ralls County. Father Landry Genosky, a priest who studied and wrote about the Toltons, said that the story varied with the state where it was told. In the Missouri version, the Toltons were freed by the Elliotts. Peter Tolton went to St. Louis to join the Union army, while Martha Jane moved north with the help of a neighbor. In the Illinois version, based on Tolton family reports, the slaves were not freed, but escaped.

The historian Goldena Howard, who searched for information about the Tolton family in the 1950s, wrote: "Some say the Elliotts freed the family, but if so, the record of manumission is lost in the spidery records of Ralls County Circuit Court, and has not been found." Elliott family oral history, posted on the Internet in 2000, says that Stephen Elliott sent Martha Jane and the children to Illinois for their protection.

At the time, there were about three hundred people in Quincy's "Negro district," and Martha Jane quickly found a place to stay, with a woman named Mrs. Davis. There was also work for the family. The Harris Tobacco Factory employed three hundred people, including many black people, in their cigar-making shop. Martha Jane, Charles, and Augustine took jobs. Augustine was paid fifty cents a week when he started, and he eventually made six dollars per week as a "stemmer," removing stems from the tobacco leaves. Mrs. Davis, who worked at night, cared for the baby, Anne, while the other Toltons worked. At night, when Mrs. Davis worked, Mrs. Tolton watched the Davis child, Mary Ann.

There were no child labor laws. Martha Jane, Charles, and Augustine worked ten hours a day, six days a week, all during the hot summer. There was no time for school, and no school for black children, but Augustine later remembered that his boss at the factory, an African American named Mr. Pleasant, was kind to him. Also, on Sundays the family could attend St. Boniface, a German Catholic church.

The mass was in Latin, with sermons in German. The pastor summarized the sermon in English. Martha Jane encouraged Augustine to learn the service and the new languages. She knew that to get an education he would have to attend the Catholic schools. By listening, Augustine picked up some Latin and German, which would serve him well later.

In the winters the cigar factory closed, and the Toltons lived on the little they had managed to save. In 1863, Charles caught pneumonia. With no access to doctors or medicines, people treated infections with homemade cures. For pneumonia, the standard care was to make a mustard paste, or mustard plaster, and apply it to the chest. Along with prayer and constant attention, this treatment sometimes defeated the disease. Martha Jane stayed by her son's bedside day and night, but her remedies failed. Charles, her firstborn son, died.

The Civil War was long and bloody, and Missouri lost many men, both black and white. The economy of the South was ruined, and it would take years for Southern and border states such as Missouri to recover. Still, on January 11, 1865, "an ordinance abolishing slavery in Missouri" made the state the first in the United States to free slaves. The right of black men to vote was achieved in 1870 when the Fifteenth Amendment to the U.S.

Constitution guaranteed the right to vote without regard to "race, color, or previous condition of servitude."

Throughout the war years, Martha Jane hoped her husband would find her—but she learned that he had died in St. Louis. His name appeared among the 63,178 African American names on the official casualty list of the Union army. Some historians believe he died in a St. Louis hospital of dysentery or measles. Martha Jane and the children were now completely dependent on one another and the network of friends they had made in Quincy.

Still hoping that Augustine could get an education, Martha Jane enrolled him in the all-white school at St. Boniface Church. Father Schaeffermeyer at St. Boniface was willing for him to begin classes, and one nun, Sister Chrysologus, planned to give the eleven-year-old extra help so he could catch up. The parents of the other children, however, did not welcome him.

St. Boniface students made fun of his accent and called him names. Before a month had passed, he left school. Father Schaeffermeyer remembered later, "I can still see them—mother and son—Mrs. Tolton's arms flung around the boy's shoulders, walking down the sidewalk after we drove them out." Three more years passed before Augustine would try school again.

At fourteen, Augustine was far behind the younger students when he enrolled at Colored School Number One in a log cabin in Quincy. He was tall, had very dark skin, and could not yet read or write. Since the family had no father at home, children whispered stories about his mother. He left school soon after he started.

With these setbacks, Martha Jane must have almost given up, but in 1868, when Mary Ann Davis was dying of tuberculosis, Martha Jane and Augustine had an opportunity to meet Father McGirr, the priest of St. Lawrence O'Toole Church. Father McGirr had come to America as a fifteen-year-old from Ireland during the potato famine. He knew what it was like to be in an unfriendly place, poor and alone. He promised Martha Jane that if Augustine would come to school at St. Lawrence there would be no trouble.

The family moved to a home close to St. Lawrence. While keeping his job at the cigar factory, Augustine was able to go to school in the winter. "As long as I was in that school, I was safe," Augustine later said, "I learned the alphabet, spelling, reading and arithmetic."

He also learned the Latin mass and began to help Father Mc-Girr. Soon it was evident that the devoted young man would be a credit to the Church, and Father McGirr set out to help him become a priest. For Martha Jane, the idea of a priest in the family must have been thrilling, but, as was always true in her life, it would be a long time until the way was clear. While she continued to support the family, Augustine studied with one priest after another.

At one point, the family moved from Illinois back to northeast Missouri. Martha Jane worked as a housekeeper for a priest named Patrick Dolan, who had lived on a farm near Father Mc-Girr's home in Ireland. Augustine worked as a custodian and got an extra job, but he was not allowed to serve at mass. The arrangement lasted less than a year. Dolan, it turned out, had a drinking problem, and Father McGirr advised them to return to Quincy at once.

Back in Quincy, Martha Jane went back to the cigar factory and Augustine took a series of jobs, working for a saddle maker and a soda bottler. Always active in the church and in the black community, he dreamed of becoming a missionary and saving souls in Africa.

In the collection of Tolton papers at Quincy University, there is an 1875 letter from Theodore Wegmann, assistant priest of St. Boniface, to a pastor in Baltimore. It asks for information "in behalf of a young man of the African race, who is very desirous of becoming a missionary for the people of his race." He continued, saying that Augustine had been "studying Latin now for over a year[;] he reads Nepos and Caesar without difficulty . . . some weeks ago I have begun Greek with him. . . . August Tolton is his name."

It is unclear if the letter was answered. If so, the answer was that the United States had no place for a black Catholic theology student. The family stayed in Quincy, and when a Franciscan priest, Father Michael Richart, began a Sunday School for African Americans in 1877, Augustine helped bring students. Father Richart wrote that Augustine was a "pious, modest and studious young man."

Soon after opening the Sunday School, Father Richart proposed to open a free day school. "Always assisted by Mr. August Tolton and his worthy mother, an accomplished lady and devoted Catholic, I soon had a schoolroom in an abandoned school-house of St. Boniface's Congregation," wrote Richart. They soon had forty students.

Augustine had developed a strong network of white priests in Quincy who cared about him and wanted to help. The priests from St. Francis College allowed him to take classes at the college, which is now Quincy University. Here, between 1878 and 1880, he began to study German, Greek, Latin, and English, and ancient, medieval, and modern history. The priests continued to look for a seminary that would help.

Finally, in 1880, the Urban College in Rome accepted Augustine. From this college, priests went as missionaries all over the world to build new churches. Augustine hoped that he would be sent to Africa. Martha Jane, while overjoyed that he had finally been admitted for advanced studies, must have been worried that she would never see him again. It was with mixed emotions that she said good-bye, wishing him well on his long journey.

Augustine signed his name "Augustus" on the college roll. He was one of 142 students from all over the world, including black students from Africa and Asians from China and Japan. "All were

Since there are no photographs of Martha Jane,
Augustine Tolton's handsome features and quiet
strength must serve as a reflection of his mother's
loving support. This photo of the young Tolton
was probably made when he was a student. The
hat, called a biretta, shows that he was educated at a
pontifical seminary. (Tolton Collection, University
Archives, Brenner Library, Quincy University.)

my friends, they all loved me, though I cannot say why," he later
told an interviewer.

On January 15, 1882, while Augustine was away, the Quincy
Catholics started a church for the black community in a building that St. Boniface's congregation purchased from a Protestant

church. Father Theodore Bruener was rector. Each Quincy congregation donated money, which was spent on carpentry, painting, vestments, and a melodeon, or reed organ.

The next year, records show that a gallery, or balcony, was built in the black church, called St. Joseph's Church, and that other repairs and school bills were paid. St. Joseph's still owed three thousand dollars to St. Boniface for the building.

Augustine was far away in Rome. He later said that his mother taught him the Ten Commandments, but she never learned to read or write. Martha Jane must have eagerly awaited news from her son, even though she depended on others to read the letters to her.

In 1886 Augustine wrote, "My seminary studies are about over now, and I will go on to Africa right after my ordination in April." He was disappointed, but his mother must have been thrilled when his teachers announced that he was to return to his parish in Quincy and minister to the people he had known.

"If America has never seen a black priest, it has to see one now," said the prefect of the Urban College, sending Augustine back to the United States. Indeed, from the time he first arrived in New York after his journey from Rome, he was enthusiastically received. He celebrated his first mass in the United States at St. Benedict the Moor Church in New York on July 11, 1886. After a mass for the Franciscan Sisters at Hoboken, New Jersey, he started his journey back to Quincy.

We can imagine that the day of Augustine's return was one of the happiest in Martha Jane's life. She and Anne must have been full of excitement and anticipation. Their own Augustine was returning to Quincy, Illinois, as the first purely black priest born in the United States. Three mixed-race brothers, the Healys, born in Georgia, had become priests between 1854 and 1864, but they had light skin and a prosperous white father, making them more acceptable to white congregations.

Black and white Catholics had planned a big welcome. Augustine's old friend and mentor, Father McGirr, arranged for a railroad car to take Quincy friends to Springfield, Illinois, to meet "Father Tolton." Rumbling across the prairie, Martha Jane and Anne would have hardly noticed the miles fly by. Augustine was coming home!

Returning to the Quincy station, the train was met by a brass band playing hymns, and Augustine was taken in a carriage drawn by four white horses to St. Peter's Church, where hundreds of people—an estimated one thousand whites and five hundred blacks—waited to receive his blessing. Augustine called his mother to him before blessing the others.

The crowds were so large that his first mass in Quincy was moved to the much larger St. Boniface Church. An estimated crowd of six hundred, including all races and denominations, had come to see him and hear him sing the mass. He thanked the many people who had helped him achieve an education. "Above all," he said, "I want to thank my mother." The newspaper reported that the Quincy congregation loved hearing the young priest's "rich, musical voice."

The newspapers said little about Augustine's mother. Still, we know that Martha Jane—now known as "Mother Tolton"—devoted herself to her son and his memory for the rest of her life.

Father Augustine was put in charge of St. Joseph's. In the financial record signed "A. Tolton" and filed February 10, 1887, he carefully recorded the details of the church purchase from St. Boniface. "Indebted to St. Boniface congregation through an agreement to sell St. Joseph's for the colored Catholics in case of success for sum of $3,000." The church had taken in $248.05.

A year later, the debt of three thousand dollars still stood, and an additional debt of one hundred dollars was noted: "To my mother (borrowed by Father Bruener 2 years before I came home)." He listed the church income as $560.40, more than twice as much as the year before Augustine came home.

In 1888, there is more detail: "$130 To my mother for putting

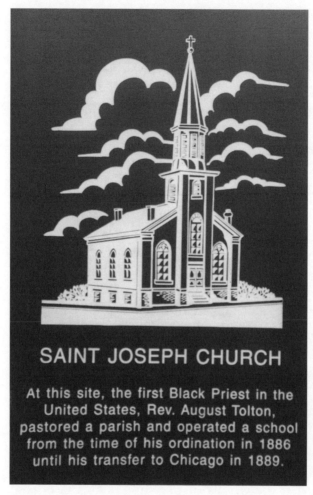

SAINT JOSEPH CHURCH

At this site, the first Black Priest in the United States, Rev. August Tolton, pastored a parish and operated a school from the time of his ordination in 1886 until his transfer to Chicago in 1889.

Saint Joseph Church in Quincy has been torn down, but this marker on the location informs visitors about the church and Father Tolton. (Photo by Father Phil Hoebing.)

up the gallery in church." Mother Tolton's $100—or $130—was probably her life savings. She must have had great faith that the church would be successful—and it wasn't long until Augustine's services drew large crowds. The church income was higher—$695.45—but not enough to repay any loans. In 1888, the *St. Joseph's Advocate* praised the new priest, saying:

And so we have in our midst today a colored priest . . . once a slave . . . said to be incapable of education, moral habits, etc.

. . . [T]he genuine article, a typical Afro-American. As our perfect facsimile of his photograph shows the vivid and striking likeness of a solid man, true as steel, without a shadow of pretension, well up in his sacred duties, able to preach and converse in more than one language, humble as a child, boasting of his African blood and aglow with devotion and love for his race. As he passes through the streets of Quincy, men raise their hats to him and the priests at table give him the place of honor. . . .

[He is t]he First and Only Native American Priest of African Descent through Both Parents On The Continent. . . . Beyond a doubt we are writing history this time, history never written before, history to stand and to be quoted. First men are necessarily historic men, most particularly in religion and race.

Father Tolton was invited to many Catholic ceremonies in the region. In the Tolton collection at Quincy University is a copy of a letter he wrote to accept the invitation for James Ryan's installation as Bishop of Alton in 1888. With characteristic wit, Tolton wrote, "So you have not forgotten the black sheep in your diocese . . . be sure that I will be present."

Tolton was very popular, but in his first year he reported only six conversions. "The majority of the Negroes here are baptists and Calvinists and many are Masons. . . . The Negroes in Chicago complain that they do not have a Negro priest and that I am here in Quincy. . . . There is also a priest here who accuses me of wasting my time."

Not only that, but his parishioners were poor. His main support came from Irish and German Catholics. Black children came to the parish school to be warm and to receive food, but they could not contribute to expenses. The first African American priest was a celebrity, and other parishes sold reproductions

The *St. Joseph's Advocate* published the story of Tolton's life from interviews with him. Its last installment explains that Tolton had objected to having his picture published. His portrait was in great demand, which he called "terrible," adding, "I never wanted them, neither for myself nor anybody else, not even for my mother, for I am here . . ." (Tolton Collection, University Archives, Brenner Library, Quincy University.)

of his picture to make money, but this did not help him with expenses.

Father Tolton earned a little money for the parish by taking outside speaking engagements, but he did not like leaving Quincy. In 1889 he was the main speaker at the First Catholic Colored Congress in Washington, D.C., preaching that "The Catholic Church deplores double slavery—that of the mind and that of the body."

At about this time, his troubles in Quincy became serious. A new priest, Father Michael Weiss, was assigned to St. Boniface Church and was also appointed as the dean or leader of the Quincy area Catholic clergy. St. Boniface was deeply in debt and Father Weiss was unhappy about his parish maintaining the building for the negro parish and especially unhappy that his parishioners often attended St. Joseph. Some sources say that white priests were jealous because Father Tolton's services were attracting so many Catholics that the support for other congregations was shrinking. Further trouble developed when the daughter of a "society matron" in Quincy was frustrated when she wanted to marry an "unacceptable" person. Her mother influenced the priests of the white churches to reject the couple, but she forgot Father Tolton.

The young bride-to-be asked Father Tolton to marry them in his church, and he performed the ceremony, making Father Weiss and others even more angry. Father Weiss persuaded the bishop to ask Augustine not to minister to white people. In a letter to the Sacred Congregation of the Propaganda in Rome, Augustine wrote, "There is a certain German priest here who is jealous and insolent. He offends me in many ways and hurts me deeply. . . . I would gladly go elsewhere just to be rid of him. . . ."

The Sacred Congregation of the Propaganda investigated; it received a letter from the bishop that said, "Father Tolton is a good priest, however he wants to establish a type of society here which is not feasible." Soon after, Tolton wrote, "I cannot endure it here any longer with this German priest." Rome gave him permission to "Just go at once."

Father Augustine, Mother Tolton, and Anne arrived in Chicago in December 1889. There, they found challenges. The 1871 Chicago Fire had destroyed the Holy Name Cathedral, and the bishop had bought an old Protestant church at Ninth and Wabash for his cathedral. It had become St. Mary's Parish, and the first Catholic service for African Americans in Chicago had been held only seven years earlier in St. Mary's basement.

The black population, while larger than Quincy's, was just as poor. Father Tolton had to build a congregation, then build a church. Almost as soon as he arrived in Chicago, he was writing back to friends in Quincy. On a card printed "Rev. A. Tolton, Rector, St. Monica's Church, Chicago," he wrote: "Katie. This is the name of my new church which I have to build. Tell Amy Heine to get big and come to Chicago."

Black Chicagoans were likely to be members of Protestant denominations such as the Baptist and African Methodist Episcopal (A.M.E.) Churches, but Chicago Catholics welcomed a church for black Catholics. Within a month of arriving in Chicago, Tolton wrote Father John R. Slattery, in Baltimore, Maryland, that he had secured a location for the church. Soon after, he received a ten-thousand-dollar donation from a wealthy white woman named Anna O'Neill to begin building St. Monica's, named for the mother of St. Augustine.

Rev. Slattery had been outspoken against Catholic prejudice against blacks and had become a missionary to American blacks. His order, called "Josephites," defended the rights of blacks to be priests. There are two letters from Tolton to Slattery in the archive at Quincy University.

The first was written just four weeks after Tolton arrived in Chicago:

I must say that I wish at this moment that there were 27 Father Toltons, or colored priests at any rate, who could supply the demands; 27 letters at this moment asking me to come and lecture, come and give my kind assistance all of them speaking in the same light . . . what a grand thing it would be if I were only a travelling missionary to go to all of the places that have called for me or what a grand thing if I were a Josephite belonging to your rank of missionaries. I could then get over America and accomplish something; but here also I am hard at work I have 27,000 to work among here. So you see I am pushed now and a lot on the brain . . .

Augustine was also quickly recruited into the planning committee for the celebration marking twenty-five years of service by Archbishop Patrick Augustine Feehan. The Silver Jubilee lasted through much of October 1890 and focused the energy of Chicago's entire Catholic community.

Tolton was one of seven priests in charge of the "Pupils' Programme." "It is the first time that so many children were brought together under one roof in this city," says a book commemorating the event, "representing many nations, speaking many languages, but all united by one Faith and under one Flag . . . with flags and banners, the girls attired in white dresses with blue, pink, red or green ribbons; the boys in dark handsome suits, manly little fellows . . ."

The program allowed twenty minutes each for presentations by African American pupils, Italian pupils, French Canadian pupils, German pupils, German orphans, Bohemian pupils, Polish pupils, deaf-mute pupils, English-speaking pupils, and pupils from St. Joseph's Orphanage and Feehanville Training School. Each speaker brought a "beautiful flower offering to his Grace," so that the stage became a bank of "rare and beautiful flowers" as the program proceeded.

Four children from St. Monica's spoke, addressing the archbishop and presenting baskets and bouquets of flowers. "Following these, a colored boy twelve years of age rendered a violin solo
in a most creditable manner; and two clever little colored boys
executed a duet on guitars that delighted the entire audience."
As in many events of the church, Martha Jane, who served as
sacristan, and Augustine must have worked together to plan the
presentation.

The final event of the celebration brought Catholics together
from all parts of Chicago into a procession. For the first time, "the
faithful of twelve distinct nationalities," including ethnic Polish,
German, Irish, and African American people, marched together
in a grand display, which one witness called "the grandest popular
pageant ever witnessed in this country." No doubt Martha Jane
was in the procession.

By 1891, the Toltons' Catholic flock numbered about thirty.
Father Tolton wrote Rev. Slattery that he was looking for black
Chicagoans for the priesthood, and that he was giving instruc-
tions to one. Tolton's desire to be a missionary never left him,
and he again expressed his wish that he could be a Josephite.

At the same time, debate was beginning on how to present
America's diversity at the approaching 1893 Chicago World's
Exposition, planned to celebrate national progress four hundred
years after Columbus's arrival in the New World. In 1890, President Benjamin Harrison appointed a national commission for
planning the World's Columbian Exposition. He named two
representatives from each state and territory and one from the
District of Columbia. The all-white, all-male commissioners appointed an all-white "Board of Lady Managers," with representatives from every state and territory and the District of Columbia.

Three days after the Lady Managers met, black women held
a meeting at Chicago's Bethesda Baptist Chapel. According to a
report by Erin Shaughnessy of the State University of New York
at Binghamton, the women debated on three points: "how Black

women should be represented at the fair; how Black Americans should be represented; and whether African-American representatives at the fair should emphasize the positive or the negative features of their contemporary social conditions in the United States."

The debate at the meeting paralleled an ongoing debate in larger society. By 1890, a few blacks had gained college educations and prominence as professionals. Those without educations could barely make a living working in the few jobs open to them—usually as domestic workers in the homes of whites or well-to-do blacks. The lack of opportunities for education and employment was a serious problem.

African Americans debated the questions of how they would fit into white America, and the Toltons must have followed the debates closely. Father Tolton's 1892 talk in Philadelphia, calling the Catholic Church "the only True Liberator of Mankind" referred to the injustice suffered by African Americans. Martha Jane and Anne would have been particularly drawn into the discussion, especially since so much of the debate centered around education, a lifelong passion for Martha Jane.

The failure of justice for blacks accused of crimes was of great concern throughout the United States. Often, lynch mobs formed as soon as a black was accused of a crime. Pursuing the accused to jail, the mobs sometimes managed to capture and hang him before a trial could be held.

The black women insisted that they be represented in planning for the exposition and finally gained the appointment on the Board of Lady Managers of African American Mrs. A. M. Curtis to be the "Secretary of Colored Interests." The wife of a black doctor, Mrs. Curtis was not representative of the majority of black Americans, and she met resistance on every side. At the same time, she claimed success in obtaining a thousand jobs in construction and maintenance for blacks and space in the women's building for an exhibit. In August at the fair, there would also be a "Colored

American Day" at the exposition to encourage African Americans to visit the exhibits.

Three African Americans submitted work to the fair board: Edmonia Lewis's sculpture *Hiawatha* graced the entrance of the women's building; George Washington Carver's painting *Yucca Glorioso* won a prize; and New Yorker Joan Imogen Howard, the only African American to serve on a state board, compiled statistics showing African American achievements.

A main attraction at the fair was an African American woman named Nancy Green, who played the part of Aunt Jemima in the exhibit of the R. T. Davis Milling Company, which produced Aunt Jemima pancake mix. Green flipped pancakes and told cheerful stories about plantation life while a salesman distributed buttons with the Aunt Jemima slogan "I'se in town, honey." This pancake mix image, called "Slave in a Box" by Maurice Manring in a book by that title, was one of the few images of African Americans seen by most white visitors to the exposition.

African American leaders expressed their opposition to the "politics of exclusion" of exposition planners in *The Reason Why the Colored American is not in the World's Columbian Exposition,* a pamphlet published in 1893 with essays by Frederick Douglass, the antilynching activist Ida B. Wells, and others discussing the accomplishments of black Americans and their continuing problems. In his essay, "The Reason Why," F. L. Barnett wrote: "In the very first steps of the Exposition Work, the colored people were given to understand they were *persona non grata.*" Later in the essay he observed that "In this wonderful hive of National Industry . . . numbering employees in the thousands, only two colored persons could be found whose occupations were of higher grade than that of janitor, laborer and porter, and these two only clerkships."

Several black women addressed the weeklong "World's Congress of Representative Women" at the exposition. Frances E. W. Harper of Virginia called for "a national education bill . . .

to secure an education to the children of those who were born under the shadow of institutions which made it a crime to read." She also pointed out the injustice of allowing lynchers to vote, and she called for votes for women. "If the fifteenth century discovered America to the Old World, the nineteenth century is discovering woman to herself," she said.

Mrs. A. J. Cooper, a black principal from Washington, D.C., discussed "The Intellectual Progress of the Colored Women of the United States since the Emancipation Proclamation." She reported that there were 25,530 colored schools in the United States and 1,353,352 pupils "of both sexes." There were 22,956 colored teachers and 247 "colored students (a large percentage of whom are women) now preparing themselves in the universities of Europe." Four American colleges had given college degrees to black women—Oberlin, Ann Arbor, Wellesley, and Cornell.

Black Chicagoan Fannie Barrier Williams spoke about discrimination against black women seeking jobs and the unpleasantness of riding in segregated train cars, which she compared to cattle cars. "Less is known of our women than of any other class of Americans," she said, adding that blacks had embraced creeds as various as Catholicism and the "no-creed of Emerson." "No church, school, or charitable institution for the special use of colored people has been allowed to languish or fail when the associated efforts of the women could save it."

These words were certainly true of the women of St. Monica's, who were working to build a church at Thirty-sixth and Dearborn. To raise money, the congregation formed the St. Augustine Society and sold tickets to dinners, socials, and fairs. Much of the fund-raising was done by women, and although they ran out of money when the building was only half-completed, St. Monica's was roofed and dedicated in 1893. The dedication was a proud moment for the congregation, and Father Tolton must have remarked on the contribution of the women. He certainly thought about his mother and what she had helped him achieve.

Father Tolton wrote to a friend, "I really feel there will be a stir all over the United States when I begin my church." St. Monica's Church was a fine stone building, designed by a black architect and built by black workmen. The building served the community until 1924 when the parish moved to nearby St. Elizabeth's. (Archives of the Archdiocese of Chicago.)

Father Tolton's congregation had grown to six hundred, and Martha Jane was busy with church work. In 1896, a priest from Iowa visited them in their small house behind St. Monica's and recorded this impression:

> They lived in a poorly furnished but very clean house. The meals were simple affairs. Father Tolton, his mother and I sat at a table having an oil cloth cover. A kerosene lamp stood in the middle.
>
> On the wall directly behind Father's place hung a large black rosary. As soon as the evening meal was over, Father Tolton would rise and take the beads from the nail. He kissed the large crucifix reverently. We all knelt on the bare floor while the Negro priest, in a low voice, led the prayers with deliberate slowness and with unmistakable fervor.

Father Tolton wore himself out working for the impoverished

community of St. Monica's. On July 9, 1897, he collapsed on the street. He may have been collecting money for the church that day or returning from a meeting of priests. It was an extremely hot day—eighty-eight degrees at eight in the morning. At least four Chicagoans died of heat strokes that day.

The *Quincy Journal* reported that at eight-thirty that evening, the forty-six-year-old Tolton had died of heat prostration at Mercy Hospital. Survivors included "his mother and his sister Mrs. B. Pettis of Chicago." Tolton's body was taken back to Quincy for burial.

The *Quincy Journal* reported that the city had rarely seen such a large funeral. The procession extended four blocks and special streetcars took people partway to the cemetery, dropping them off to walk. Among the pallbearers were friends, black and white, from Quincy and Chicago.

Martha Jane, Anne, and Anne's husband accompanied the body from Chicago. Father Tolton was buried in the center of Saint Peter's cemetery, otherwise an all-white cemetery. Since there was no space reserved for him, he was buried in the plot reserved for Father John Patrick Kerr. When Kerr died on March 2, 1914, he was buried above Tolton. The cross marking the grave is inscribed on both sides, with Tolton's name on the east side and Kerr's on the west. Tolton's inscription reads:

> Rev. Augustine Tolton
> The First Colored Priest In United States
> Born at Brush Creek, Ralls County, Missouri
> April 1, 1854
> Ordained in Rome April 24, 1886
> Died July 9, 1897
> Requiescat in Pace.

Martha Jane returned to Chicago, where Anne had settled and married. An Irish priest was put in charge of St. Monica's, but Martha Jane continued to serve as sacristan there. Although she saw the parish grow, it never prospered. Barred from joining labor unions, African American men were limited to the lowest-paying jobs, and African American women almost never found employment beyond being domestic servants.

Martha Jane died in 1911, and the next year St. Monica's became a convent and school for black children. According to records from the Archdiocese of Chicago, its "small chapel" was in 1920 "the only place of divine worship for the colored Catholics in Chicago Diocese."

In 1924, the parish was combined with St. Elizabeth's. As Father Roy Bauer later wrote, Father Tolton's mother was spared seeing St. Monica's end.

Researchers have located no record in Quincy or Chicago to tell us Martha Jane's burial place or what happened to Anne. One researcher believes that Anne left the Catholic Church and became a pastor of an A.M.E. Church in Connecticut.

Often, a mother's courage springs from the wish that the future will be better for the next generation. This wish powered Martha Jane as she led her children to freedom, and she inspires those who know of her today.

## FOR MORE READING

Unfortunately, the books written about slave women, especially Missouri slave women, are few. One landmark study is *Celia, a Slave,* by Melton A. McLaurin (Athens: University of Georgia Press, 1991; there is also a 1999 paperback edition from Bard Books). Purchased at the age of fourteen as both a slave and concubine, in 1855 Celia took revenge on her Callaway County owner by murdering him. She was tried, convicted, and hanged for the crime.

The narratives of some slave women appear in *To Be a Slave,* compiled by Julius Lester with illustrations by Tom Feelings (1968; 30th anniversary ed., New York: Dial Books, 1998). Written for general readers, it draws from oral histories recorded in the 1930s and stored in the National Archives; Lester also adds historical data to give context to the slaves' statements. Unfortunately, none of the informants was from Missouri.

There is a biography of Augustus Tolton in the *Dictionary of Missouri Biography* (Columbia: University of Missouri Press, 1999). The entry says little about his mother.

In 1993, Father Roy Bauer, Pastor of Saint Peter Church in Quincy, Illinois, wrote *They Called Him Father Gus: The Life and Times of August Tolton, First Black Priest in the U.S.A.* The booklet focuses on Augustine, but it barely touches on the life of his mother.

# 4

## *Nell Donnelly Reed*

You can't be a well-balanced person if you insist on devoting all your attention to business, even those details which can be managed by others, leaving no time free for your development as a human being.

—Nell Donnelly Reed, to a reporter

Nell Donnelly Reed gained national recognition by boldly rejecting the boring, unflattering housedresses worn by most women of her time and turning an eye for fashion into a multi-million-dollar business. She was respected as a successful businesswoman, humanitarian, loving mother of an adopted son, and avid outdoorswoman. She became widely known for her generosity and good business practices; she was one of the first employers in the United States to offer improved working conditions, medical services, and group hospitalization benefits for her employees.

Born Ellen Quinlan on March 6, 1889, on a farm in Parsons, Kansas, Nell was the twelfth of thirteen children. Her father, a farmer and railroad worker, had emigrated from County Cork, Ireland, hoping to find a better life in the United States. Nell received her education at a local Catholic convent, and after she graduated from high school, she moved to Kansas City and took a job as a stenographer. She found a rooming house where she could live and soon met Paul J. Donnelly, who also lived there. They were married when Nell was seventeen.

The young couple saved money from their joint earnings so that Nell could go to Lindenwood College in St. Charles, Missouri. Few women went to college in those days, and it was even more rare for a woman to attend college after marriage. In fact, Nell was the only married student at Lindenwood. Paul Donnelly explained later to a reporter that he had "always sensed that Nell was intelligent."

Nell graduated from Lindenwood College in 1909 and returned home so that she and Paul could start their life together in Kansas City. They had no children, which gave Nell time to enjoy her lifelong passion for sewing. At that time, women working at home usually wore shapeless sixty-seven-cent housedresses. The thinking seemed to be that if a woman spent most of her time cleaning and looking after children, it was a waste of money and effort for her to wear attractive clothes at home.

Nell had an entirely different approach. She often remarked to her classmates at Lindenwood that she was determined to look presentable all the time, even if she were confined to working at home for most of her life. Her mother and sisters had taught her to sew when she was young, and she excelled at it, never needing to use a pattern. Using high-quality fabrics that would not fade or fall apart, Nell created a wide array of stylish, flattering dresses and aprons for herself and for her family. Her dresses, which were form-fitting but never tight, usually reached to the knees and were pleated to allow for comfortable movement. The sleeves, which were often adjustable, were fairly short, also allowing for increased movement. One Christmas, she made brightly colored, tasteful dresses for all of her sisters.

Soon, Nell's neighbors and friends were asking where she had gotten such beautiful clothing. When she told them she sewed her own dresses, they insisted that she make more that they could purchase. Nell collected their measurements and went to work. She had never thought of herself as a dressmaker, but she soon realized that there might be a market for her skills. Her friends and neighbors loved the dresses and suggested that she take samples to a department store.

Nell was not sure if store managers would welcome her clothing and accept her as a business associate, or if they would laugh at her. After all, it was 1916, and it was not customary for a woman to start a business. However, she decided to investigate her market. She checked around Kansas City stores looking for affordable, attractive housedresses, but she could not find any. It seemed that women had two choices. They could either pay a fortune for designer clothing, or they could wear the "Old Mother Hubbard" style of apparel—shapeless and unflattering, designed like a sack, and with few choices in color.

Nell thought that she may have found a niche in the market. So she got up the courage to take a few of her designs to the George C. Peck Dry Goods Company. Peck's was a leading Kansas City department store—a huge building in a prominent location. Nell feared that they might not take her seriously, but the buyer said he would take eighteen dozen dresses.

Nell was astounded. When she got home, she told Paul about the large order, that she was thinking of starting a dressmaking company, and that she would need some money to start it. Paul had often talked about starting a small business of his own but had never thought it would involve making dresses for women. However, Nell was able to convince him that her idea was worth a try. Paul backed her with $1,270 of his savings.

Nell used Paul's money and some of her own savings to purchase two power sewing machines, which she set up in the attic. Then she hired two seamstresses to fill the order for Peck's. The dresses were priced at one dollar, a high price in those days. However, Peck's sold out of all 216 dresses the first morning they were on the racks. These first sales were the founda-

In a 1931 interview for *Independent Woman* magazine, Nell remarked, "I've heard some women say that they would rather talk with men, have business dealings with men. I don't feel that way about it. I have no preference or prejudice in the matter. I like to talk business with a competent person, whether that person is a man or a woman." (Western Historical Manuscript Collection–Kansas City.)

tion for the largest dressmaking business of the early twentieth century.

Nell and Paul used fifteen hundred dollars to open a small factory in downtown Kansas City, Missouri, on the corner of Twenty-ninth Street and Brooklyn Avenue. The business soon outgrew the location. In 1918, before Paul enlisted for service near the end of World War I, they moved the company into the former Coca Cola building at Twenty-first Street and Grand Avenue. When Paul returned from the war, Nell's company had already achieved such growth that he decided to leave his job as credit manager of the Barton Shoe Company in Kansas City and join her on a full-time basis.

Paul took the position of president, and Nell became the secretary-treasurer. The titles were misleading, however. Paul was in charge of the financial affairs, but Nell designed the dresses, hired the workers, and supervised sales. She studied the market to find out where her clothes were being worn and by whom. She traveled to Paris and Vienna for inspiration, new designs, and the best fabrics she could find. Under her watchful eye, the fabrics were rigorously tested for color fastness, quality, and durability.

The Donnelly Garment Company thrived throughout the 1920s, in some years grossing as much as $3.5 million. It consistently offered durable, attractive clothing that was affordable even on a tight budget. One of Nell's primary concerns was that her garments fit the women who purchased them, so that the purchaser would not have to spend money on alterations. Before any design went into production, Nell required that a sample be made for every size. Then, each sample was tested on a model of the size and age group the dress was intended for. If the dress did not fit properly, the pattern would be reworked.

The public took notice. In 1927, Nell was voted Kansas City's most illustrious businesswoman. By 1931, the Donnelly Garment Company had a thousand employees, and Nell's garments were becoming well known on the east and west coasts.

Nell was concerned with her company's financial bottom line and with the quality of her dresses, but her sense of responsibility did not end there. She wanted to improve the well-being of her workers. There had been a terrible fire in a New York dressmaking factory in 1911. The workers were trapped in the ninth-floor Triangle Shirtwaist Factory and died in the blaze or jumped to their deaths. A hundred and forty-six lost their lives, mostly girls and women.

Investigators found that the workers had been crowded into the stifling shop with the doors locked so they could not leave work. The locked doors had prevented their escape. This well-publicized fire probably motivated Nell to provide the best pos-

Nell Donnelly Reed's factory at 1828 Walnut in Kansas City grew to an entire city block. Modern and innovative, she looked for new technology to assist the manufacturing process. Nell was the first to adopt a production method called a "ski run." After the garments were sewn, they were brought to the pressing and inspection rooms, then transported by a conveyor to a lower floor, checked again, packed, and sent to stores. (Western Historical Manuscript Collection–Kansas City.)

sible working conditions she could for her employees. Donnelly Garment Company employees were among the first to have safe working conditions, access to medical care, and generous wages for the time. Nell also believed that her employees and their children deserved educational opportunities. She offered to pay for her employees, who were mostly women, to attend night classes. She even offered her employees' children scholarships to local colleges.

The success Nell and Paul enjoyed throughout the 1920s was not shared by all the world. As the decade drew to a close, the United States, as well as Europe and other industrialized nations, headed into the period of economic distress known as the

In 1931, Nell told a reporter for the magazine *Independent Woman,* "The attitude of our employees towards the executives in the firm is not that they have to work *under* others, but that they are working with others." (Western Historical Manuscript Collection–Kansas City.)

Great Depression. For three years after the Stock Market crash of October 1929, stock prices on the New York Stock Exchange dropped steadily. Everyone with money in the stock market, including private investors, financial institutions, and the corporations themselves, was affected. By 1932, manufacturing output in the United States was half what it had been in 1929. More than a fifth of the workforce was unemployed. Europe, heavily dependent on the United States for loans and postwar economic aid, was also deeply affected.

In this time of financial upheaval, Nell's wealth and fame made her a target for criminals. At 6 P.M. on December 16, 1931, Nell and her chauffeur were returning to the Donnelly home at 5255 Oak Street in Kansas City when they were kidnapped by three men. Nell reported to police later that her abductors were waiting in a small car that pulled in and blocked her driveway just as her chauffeur, George Blair, had driven in. One man had a gun and got into the car next to Blair in the front seat. He tied Blair's hands and feet and started driving. The other two men had already climbed into the backseat with Nell and, after struggling for several blocks, finally forced her to the floor. For nearly an hour she was held on the back floorboard, unable to see anything.

The men took Nell and her chauffeur to a dingy, four-room cottage in Bonner Springs, Kansas. Nell was forced to lie on a cot, guarded, while Blair was blindfolded and bound hand and foot. Nell told police later that the walls of the house were covered with religious pictures. Police learned later that the twenty-acre farm was rented to twenty-nine-year-old Paul Scheidt, who worked the land and operated a cream station for Aines Farm Dairy.

The next morning, Paul Donnelly received a letter from Nell's kidnappers demanding seventy-five thousand dollars. They threatened that if he didn't pay they would blind Nell and kill her chauffeur. Paul was not to tell the police or any other authorities about the kidnapping. If the news got out, the kidnappers would blind Nell and kill the driver on the spot.

Paul Donnelly did not call the police. Instead, he called his lawyer, James E. Taylor. Taylor's wife had actually taken a message the previous evening from Nell's kidnappers. They said that

Mrs. Donnelly's car had been abandoned at Kansas City's Country Club Plaza, a busy new shopping district south of the downtown area. Taylor had disregarded the message as a practical joke meant for someone else.

When Taylor received the phone call from Paul Donnelly, he realized that the message had been no joke and the situation was indeed serious. No one had seen Nell since six o'clock the previous evening. Taylor called his law partner, James A. Reed, who was working on a lawsuit in Jefferson City. Reed, a well-known attorney and politician, was a next-door neighbor and good friend of the Donnellys.

Early in his career, James Reed had forged an important alliance with political bosses Jim and Tom Pendergast. Jim Pendergast had used his West Bottoms saloon as a base of operations for organizing Kansas City's powerful Democratic machine, and his brother Tom was his successor. With the friendship of the most powerful men in Kansas City on his side, James Reed had served as Kansas City counselor, Jackson County attorney, two terms as Kansas City mayor, and three as a U.S. senator.

Reed was not without critics, though. He was scorned by women's rights activists far and wide for his five-hour speech against women's suffrage when the issue came before the Senate in 1919. New women voters organized a "Rid-Us-of-Reed Club" to campaign against him in 1922. Nevertheless, he won a third term in the Senate. In 1928, he decided not to run for a fourth Senate term but to seek the Democratic nomination for president. When Al Smith won the nomination, Reed returned to private life and his law practice.

When James Reed received word of the kidnapping from Taylor, he immediately consulted with the judge of the case he had been working on. The judge granted him leave, and Reed rushed to Kansas City. Rumors about Reed's sudden departure circulated throughout the courthouse. People knew that there was trouble with the Donnelly family, but they thought that something had happened to the Donnellys' newly adopted son, David, who was only fourteen weeks old. When rumors surfaced in Jefferson City that Nell had been kidnapped, the police in Kansas City got word of it. Later that day, the *Kansas City Star*'s front-page headline read "Kidnap 'Nelly Don.'"

When Taylor, Reed, and Kansas City police chief Lewis M. Siegfried convened at Nell's home, Paul Donnelly showed them the note he had received. It was written by Nell, he explained, but it was not composed by her—the grammar and wording were poor, and the thoughts seemed disorganized:

> Dear Paul, These men say they want $75,000. Use your own judgment. They kidnapped me and chauffeur Wednesday night. If you do not pay as directed, $75,000 in cash: $25,000 in $20 bills, $25,000 in tens and $25,000 in fifties. If he or any does not do as directed we shall take him same as we have taken you. If reported to police or any authorities we shall blind you and kill nigger.

The letter ended, "Paul, yourself shall drive the car meaning our Lincoln at all times. If this letter is given to any police authorities it will be the last of me and they will get you the same way they got me."

Paul Donnelly was instructed to stop the car in front of the Mercer Hotel at Twelfth and McGee Streets at ten o'clock on December 17 and remain there for fifteen minutes to show that he was prepared to comply with the demands. If no one appeared, he was to come again the next day. If there was still no sign of the kidnappers, he was to appear the third day. After that, one of the kidnappers would start communicating with him about where he should make payments.

Taylor received a second letter, also in Nell's handwriting, stating, "I hereby give you the power to draw the money required against my husband's account to the amount of $75,000. I sign my name in full—Nell Donnelly."

When the police arrived to inspect Nell's car, which had been left behind the Plaza Movie Theatre, precisely where the caller had said it would be, they found signs of Nell's struggle. Her umbrella was in the front seat, her gloves on the back floorboard along with a coil of small rope, apparently ordinary clothesline. Her purse, hat, and a crumpled checkbook, which appeared to be smeared with blood, were on the backseat. On the floor of the green 1928 Lincoln convertible sedan was a mixture of ordinary gravel and hardened earth.

Because the kidnapping was becoming heavily publicized, James Reed stepped forward to make a statement to the kidnappers. The *Kansas City Star* published the message:

> If these men release or deliver Mrs. Donnelly unharmed, they can get their $75,000. They can get it in any form they desire and under any conditions they name. In this I am speaking for Mr. Donnelly and I add my personal guarantee. On the other hand, if a single hair on Mrs. Donnelly's head is harmed, I will, and Mr. Donnelly will spend the rest of our lives running the culprits to earth and securing for them the extreme penalty of law, which in Missouri is death by hanging.

The people of Kansas City followed the Donnelly case closely, appalled that this crime had been committed against such a prominent and beloved resident of Kansas City. Some speculated that Nell had been abducted by gangsters. However, the *Kansas City Star* reported that a member of the Kansas City underworld stepped forth and spoke with Police Chief Siegfried. The man did not reveal his identity, but he was later revealed to be John Lazia. Lazia was influential in business and political circles, and was indeed a well-known member of Kansas City's underworld.

With his connections, he would order his own unofficial search for the kidnappers.

In his conversation with Chief Siegfried, Lazia declared that knowing of Nell Donnelly's standing, political connections, and the fact that she was represented legally by Mr. Reed, no Kansas City gangster would kidnap her. An article from an unknown publication found in Nell's own personal files reported that Lazia sent twenty-five carloads of known criminals and gangsters "from underworld dive to underworld dive," armed and ready to extort information and find clues pertaining to the kidnapping. The article, "How Gangsters Solved the Donnelly Kidnapping," stated that the Kansas City police did not protest this action. They just wanted Nell to be released as soon as possible.

Nell and her chauffeur were rescued after thirty-four hours by an unknown man from Lazia's crew. The group had stopped at an all-night filling station, where the rescuer called Chief Siegfried. The police did not find Nell at the all-night filling station, but instead at an all-night candy shop with a group of people crowded around her and her chauffeur. One story reported that Nell had kept a towel from the farmhouse, and that laundry markings on the towel helped police to trace the kidnappers.

Nell told the police that the rescue had come from a group of armed men who forced their way into the house where she was being held and took her guards outside. The mysterious rescuers informed her that they could be trusted and were taking her home. After Nell's return, Chief Siegfried made the following statement to the *Kansas City Star:* "The heat was applied by the police and others, plenty of others. . . . The kidnappers found they had something too hot to handle and they turned loose."

Some people believed that Nell's kidnapping was a publicity stunt staged by the Donnellys in order to generate national recognition for their clothing line or for Senator Reed. The publicity would not, however, have helped Reed. If anything, the newspaper stories publicized his ties to Kansas City mobsters. The

*Hutchinson (Kansas) News* reported on December 22, 1931, that after learning of Nell's captivity, Reed

> hastened home, telephoned to his political friend Tom Pen-
> dergast, boss of the north side, and said he'd appreciate return
> of Mrs. Donnelly. Boss . . . said O.K., shifted his cigar, called
> the henchmen, passed the word along that Mrs. Donnelly
> should be returned and there you are. . . . It just means that
> the Kansas City police department, like all metropolitan police
> departments, is in close touch with the underworld, and that
> there has been a breach of underworld-police etiquette and
> that to correct the situation and apologize, the underworld
> boys will now aid the police in finding the kidnappers.

Soon after her kidnapping and release, Nell divorced Paul Donnelly and bought his 50 percent share of the Donnelly Garment Company. She was now the sole owner and executive director of the business. At the time, the company took up five floors of the Corrigan building and a floor of the Shukert building, both in Kansas City. It also had offices in the Empire State Building in New York. The business was worth 3.25 million dollars.

Reed acted as special prosecutor in the case against kidnapper Paul Scheidt, who testified that a farmer named William Lancey Brown of Holliday, Kansas, had approached him with the prospect of kidnapping Nell. Brown introduced Scheidt to Martin Depew. Depew's wife had formerly served in the Donnelly home as a nurse for Paul, who had been ill and under the care of a doctor and nurses for several weeks.

Scheidt insisted that he was under the impression that an oilman, who had a wealthy but stingy wife, was arranging the kidnapping in order to extort money from her. Scheidt testified that once he became aware of the true situation, he set Nell and her chauffeur free.

The jury believed the story. County Prosecutor James R. Page was astonished when Scheidt was acquitted, and he later told the

*Kansas City Star,* "It is the greatest miscarriage of justice since I have been in office. When a man can come into court and admit he is guilty of kidnapping and a jury turns him loose, it appears as if the law-abiding people haven't any protection against the criminal element."

Kidnappers Martin Depew and Walter Werner, on the other hand, were not quite so lucky. Authorities caught them after they fled to South Africa, and they both served life sentences in prison for the kidnapping, insisting the whole time that Scheidt had been aware of the true nature of the kidnapping. Another suspect, Charles Mele, was also charged, convicted, and sentenced to thirty-five years in prison for his part in the crime.

Mele insisted that he had been convicted only because of Nell's powerful political connections. "Pure political influence and nothing else. I don't know anyone connected with the case," Mele said. In fact, the jury did base its verdict on Nell's identification of Mele as one of the kidnappers. "There certainly was no reason to doubt the word of a woman of her reputation," said Daniel F. Elliot, the foreman of the jury. During the Mele trial, such a large crowd of people gathered in the courtroom that half of them were forced to stand.

The papers reported that Nell herself thanked the jurors and assured them that they had not made a mistake. Reed shook hands with each of them. The *Morning Kansas Citian* reported Nell's statement: "The verdict was as it should have been. This thing of kidnapping people is one of the worst crimes possible. I hope the manner in which this gang is being brought to justice will act as a deterrent not only here, but all through the nation."

Two years after the kidnapping, and months after the highly publicized trials, Nell's life took yet another turn. James Reed's wife had died in 1932, and, in mid-December of 1933, the newspaper society pages of Kansas City reported about a special dinner Nell Donnelly had in her home in Kansas City for her closest friends. At this dinner, on December 13, she waited for her guests to finish their meals, then requested the services of one dinner guest, the honorable Judge John C. Pollock. Everyone was asked to rise and witness an impromptu wedding ceremony. At the end of the evening, Nell and James A. Reed had become husband and wife. James Reed was seventy-two and Nell was forty-four.

Reed and Nell shared a great love of nature. She had always enjoyed the outdoors and riding horses, but he taught her to hunt and fish. When the family went on vacation to their ranch in Osconda County, Michigan, as they did frequently, Nell often took along her design team. During the day she held meetings, developed designs, and heard progress reports. However, at five o'clock everyone, including Nell, stopped working and went fishing. For fifteen years Nell held the record (ten pounds) for northern pike caught in the lake at the family ranch.

In 1937, the Donnelly Garment Company was one of the few mass-production clothing factories that had not unionized. Many textile workers, prompted by unsafe working conditions, sweatshop pay, unreasonable speedups, and long hours, had organized to fight for better representation in the workplace. After the Triangle Shirtwaist fire, strikers had held the first big protest against shirtwaist and dress manufacturers. Consisting mostly of recent eastern European immigrant women, "the Uprising of Twenty Thousand" formed the International Ladies Garment Workers Union (ILGWU). The union was able to establish a fifty-two-hour workweek, wage increases, and widespread public support.

However, when the union approached the Donnelly Garment Manufacturing Company almost thirty years later, neither Nell nor her employees were interested in signing. They resisted the ILGWU's efforts, announcing that they *already* worked under safe and healthy conditions and received excellent benefits. If they wanted to go to school, Nell paid for it. If their children wanted to go to school, Nell paid for it. If they needed medical attention, her plans offered assistance and free hospitalization. Nell's employees felt that they already had representation in the workplace and did not welcome the interference of a large national union.

In 1937, the ILGWU began a campaign to unionize against their will the employees of the Donnelly Garment Manufacturing Company. Newspapers reported that ILGWU president David Dubinsky launched the campaign as an attack on his political enemy, James A. Reed. The year before, the Democratic Party had disagreed on how to end the Depression. Reed, whom the *New York Times* called a "Jeffersonian Democrat," had led a faction of Democrats who rejected President Roosevelt's New Deal plan. At the same time, Dubinsky had helped found the American Labor Party to support the New Deal.

Roosevelt won a stunning victory in the election, and Reed and others feared that unions were part of a conspiracy that would bring communism to the United States. Actually, Dubinsky was strongly anticommunist, but he had been born in Polish Russia, making him an easy target for Reed and his followers. Now Reed was practicing law in Kansas City and married to Nell, but the bitter dispute was not forgotten. Dubinsky directed the ILGWU to set aside a hundred thousand dollars to force the unionization of Nell's company.

Nell also considered Dubinsky a communist and refused to sign an agreement with the ILGWU, which had already unionized most of the garment manufacturers in Kansas City. The ILGWU began purchasing advertisement space in national newspapers and used it to imply that Nell did not want to meet the high workplace standards of the union. One full-page advertisement appearing simultaneously in the *Kansas City Times,* the *Kansas City Star,* and the *Kansas City Post* read:

> The ILGWU cannot, should not, and will not permit one individual employer to segregate himself from the rest of the industry in the matters of work conditions and other fundamentals of employment.

In this photo, strikers picket at another garment factory in Kansas City. Despite not being unionized, most workers at Nelly Don liked their jobs. (Western Historical Manuscript Collection–Kansas City.)

The advertisement also accused Nell's employees of violating the National Labor Relations Act, commonly known as the Wagner Act, which established a legal basis for labor unions. The Wagner Act, passed by Congress in 1936, set up collective bargaining as a matter of national policy allowed by the law. It also provided for secret ballot elections for choosing unions and protected union members from employer intimidation and coercion.

In response to the ILGWU's accusations, Nell's fourteen hundred employees formed the Donnelly Garment Workers' Union on May 7, 1937. On May 11, the *Lamar (Missouri) Republican* published the statement of the Donnelly Union president, Rose

Todd: "We intend to protect our jobs and keep the right kind of working conditions. We do not need the help of outsiders to accomplish these things." Todd also told the *Maryville (Missouri) Daily Forum* that it would take more than $100,000 to force the Donnelly workers into unionization. As a result, on June 3, 1937, the ILGWU raised $250,000 to force the plant into unionization.

In the James A. Reed collection at the Western Historical Manuscripts Collection–Kansas City, boxes of documents sketch the years of bitter battle between the Donnelly Company and ILGWU. A letter dated June 30, 1937, from an ILGWU official to Swartzburg Department Store asks the store to drop the Nelly Don line and offers to prepare "a simple and direct letter that you can send to your customers explaining to them why you are no longer carrying the Nelly Don dress." The union used every tactic at its disposal—ads in the paper, brochures, attacks on James Reed, and massive letter-writing campaigns—to unionize Donnelly's.

In 1939, federal judge Andrew Miller "permanently and perpetually enjoined the Union from interfering with the company's operations in any way," but the ruling was overturned on a technicality, and the struggle continued.

While Nell was doing battle with David Dubinsky and his union, a much larger conflict was brewing abroad. Adolf Hitler, who had come to power in Germany in 1933, was secretly building up Germany's military forces, even though the Treaty of Versailles following World War I had strictly prohibited Germany from rearming. Hitler and his extremely nationalistic and anti-Semitic National Socialist Party, the Nazis, occupied the demilitarized Rhineland in 1936. Benito Mussolini, the fascist dictator of Italy, allied himself with Hitler later that year, forming a Rome-Berlin "axis." By 1939, Hitler's troops had incorporated Austria into Germany and had annexed Czechoslovakia, and Italy had annexed Albania. However, when Hitler invaded Poland on September 1, 1939, he suddenly found himself at war with Great

Britain and France. Japan joined Germany and Italy as an ally in 1940. In June 1941, Germany invaded Russia.

The United States remained neutral until December 1941, when Japan attacked the United States at Pearl Harbor and in the Philippines. The United States immediately declared war on Japan. Germany declared war on the United States, which then joined the Allied powers France, Great Britain, Russia, and China. With World War II raging on two fronts, the Donnelly Garment Manufacturing Company produced over seven million garments for the United States military.

At the same time, the company continued to make dresses. Before the war, Nell's salesmen had traveled the country in their cars with wardrobe trunks of dresses to show and take orders. A Dale Carnegie newspaper column of April 10, 1943, reported that because of war rationing the salesmen could no longer get gasoline for their cars, so Nelly Don had the factory sew miniature dresses, had the tiny dresses packed in suitcases made to look like wardrobe trunks, and sent the salesmen off by bus.

Nell's optimistic creativity was an inspiration to others who wished to start their own businesses, but she came to believe that times had changed for the worse since she started her company. In 1944 the Donnelly Garment Company was nominated in a "New Enterprise Contest" sponsored by *Reader's Digest*. A letter from Nell to the magazine reflected her feelings about labor laws and the tactics of the ILGWU: "Today, if an employer does any 'productive work,' our Supreme Court says his place of business can be picketed and that the pickets can go so far as to make untrue and defamatory statements about him." She felt that by the 1940s the only opportunity open to the average American was to establish "eating houses on important highways in the middle west and south. . . . But why indulge in such dreams when an owner can do no 'productive work' without running the risk of being . . . slandered to the extent of having his business destroyed."

Although Nell's Company earned $14 million a year during World War II making uniforms for the military, at the same time, her sales force continued to travel the country selling dresses. (Western Historical Manuscript Collection–Kansas City.)

During and after World War II, women entered the workforce in increasing numbers, some taking on occupations previously considered closed to them. When the Nelly Don line held a fashion breakfast in San Francisco in 1949, the *San Francisco Chronicle* reported that the company was particularly interested in the new, young businesswoman. Sara Pennoyer, a spokeswoman for the Nelly Don campaign, stated, "A girl's first job is herself, and she is more successful if she looks appropriately dressed for all occasions, including the 9 to 5 routine." Pennoyer continued, "Today, the inexpensive dress is the important dress. Business girls pay a larger percentage of their budget for clothes than any other group of women, research shows, and it is our business to help them look as smart as possible for as little as possible." By then, the Nelly Don factory in Kansas City had grown to be the largest of its kind in the world and was also producing accessories, such as scarves, hats, and inexpensive jewelry.

Nell's clothing was found in many large, fashionable stores, including Bloomingdale's in New York City. Nelly Don garments were always fairly priced, but never boring—and neither were the fashion exhibitions. Fashion shows were often held at the company's New York offices in the Empire State Building. For one spring show, a woman modeled a pale lilac dress with a large French poodle dyed to match at her side.

Nell was sensitive to the needs of larger women and often took styles designed for slim women and modified them to flatter larger figures. The *New York Herald-Tribune* reported in 1950, "Since the firm turns out a million and a half dresses a year, Nelly Don has to think of all the answers she can. Short sleeves this summer have turn-down arrangements for women who don't like to wear bare arms. Dresses have two waistlines, and if you're the long-waisted type, you can just rip away the upper seam." A reporter from the *New York Times,* observing the Nelly Don shows, also appreciated this attention to detail. "A coral pique had its dress straps finished with looped tabs that

Even the *New Yorker* had something to say about Nelly Don dresses, calling them part of the "how-do-they-do-it-at-the-price field," noting such innovations as deep hems, deep seams, and couturier touches. (Western Historical Manuscript Collection–Kansas City.)

not only lent ornamentation but cleverly held slip and bra straps in place."

At the same time, the firm remained in tune with women who chose more traditional occupations, such as schoolteacher and mother. For them, the Nelly Don line produced stylish clothing like the suits worn by career girls, but made in dark prints and washable fabrics. The attractive, comfortable dresses had deep armholes, soft shoulders, and fabric that allowed for leaning down and picking up objects and children.

Nell hired many women for executive positions. Although the *Kansas City Star* reported in 1932 that the company employed nine hundred women and one hundred men and that many of its female employees earned five times as much as young men of the same age, Nell insisted that her hiring policy had nothing to do with the women's rights movement. "We simply pick the person who is available, and who we believe can do the job. If that person's a woman, well and good."

She found that women could do the job. The factory and production manager had started out as a clerical worker in the payroll department. When Nell noticed her hard work and efficiency, she asked her to assist in keeping the factory's production records. From there, she worked her way up to an executive position. The woman in charge of advertising had started out as a stenographer. And Nell's own chief assistant and designer had bought Nelly Don garments for her own small shop before taking a job with the company.

Everything that happened in Nell's life drew front-page attention. When kidnapper Paul Scheidt was freed, everybody knew about it and several were outraged. When she divorced her husband and married James A. Reed, everybody read about it, and the newspaper reporters hinted that they had expected the marriage all along.

The fact that her life was so heavily publicized provides an interesting study of how the media has treated successful women. For instance, when Nell visited Tucson, Arizona, in 1951, the headline of the *Arizona Daily Star* read: "Nelly Don, Pioneer Fashion Designer, Visits in Tucson." Her success story, according to the paper, began thirty-five years before when she "became the bride of the late Senator James A. Reed" and started a dress company.

Of course, Nell had married Reed many years after she had made a name for herself in the fashion industry. Mr. Reed never took part in running Nell's company and said so in many public statements. The same article in the Tucson paper went on to report Nell was "slightly built, size 16, with blue eyes and a fair complexion." Papers generally did not describe in such detail equivalent statistics of men visiting town.

First and foremost, Nell Donnelly Reed was known as a diligent and astute businesswoman, because that is what she truly was. The Donnelly Garment Company survived and flourished during the Great Depression, and in the decade after World War II, her company became the world's largest women's ready-to-wear company under one roof. NBC Radio presented her story in 1950 in *The Golden Needle,* starring Dorothy McGuire as Nell Donnelly.

Although Nell was extremely devoted to her business, she did not allow it to take over her life. She never missed a hunting season except for 1944, the year James Reed died. For an article written by Suzanne Wilson for the *Missouri Conservationist,* Nell's son, David Q. Reed, recalled when Nell caught a six-and-a-half-pound smallmouth bass at the family ranch in Michigan. A friend of hers doubted the report, saying that smallmouth never grew beyond three and a half pounds. So Nell invited that friend to dinner, and when he arrived he saw, in the center of the dinner table, beautifully encased in ice, Nell's bass.

In 1952, Nell donated 731 acres in southern Jackson County, Missouri, to the Missouri Department of Conservation in memory of her husband. Once an expansive prairie, the property had been used for row crops and grazing. Under the Conservation Department, the land has returned to its natural state. According to the department, the James A. Reed Conservation Area now provides habitat to dozens of native animal species. An estimated ten thousand migrating geese stop over at a time, and the area has a resident flock of Canada geese. The deer population has also flourished.

The Conservation Department has worked to establish new, more sustainable growth to support the wildlife. Oaks, pecans, and walnut trees are abundant; four hundred acres of grain, much left standing, supplements the food supply for animals and birds.

Nell watched the conservation area gradually return to a more natural state, offering a refuge to the wildlife that had lost its habitat to the developments of suburban sprawl. She often returned to the area, accompanied by her chauffeur and personal secretary. Occasionally, she would bring a picnic lunch and spend the afternoon strolling around and perhaps visiting Lake Nell, which is stocked with largemouth and striped bass, channel cat, bluegill, and sunfish. On one occasion, she noticed a few bits of trash. She spoke to the person in charge of maintenance, and the debris was quickly removed.

In 1956, Nell sold her shares of the Donnelly Garment Company and left the dressmaking business. The company name was changed to Nelly Don, Inc., and in 1958 its shares were offered for trade on the open market. The new owners, however, could not keep the company profitable and eventually filed for bankruptcy.

Nell continued to be known for her social altruism. She was an active member of the Kansas City Women's Chamber of Commerce and served on the boards of Lindenwood College, the Kansas City Art Institute, and Starlight Theatre Association. Nell also served on the Kansas City Board of Education for twelve years, championing the same ideals that made her a brilliant and progressive businesswoman.

Nell continued to insist, just as when she was running her business, that education was of utmost importance. As a member of the Board of Education, she lobbied to improve the public school system. She believed it was imperative that teachers and employees of the Kansas City School District be well chosen and well treated and that they work under the best conditions, in the best facilities, with the highest pay the city could afford.

In 1951, Nell became the first woman elected to the Board of Trustees of Midwest Research Institute. Fifty years later, at the age of 101, she received the Lifetime Career Achievement Award from the Career Club of Metropolitan Kansas City.

Nell was also a devoted mother to David, who was adopted by James Reed after their marriage. David attended Princeton from 1950 to 1952, leaving to join the army. When he returned from his tour, he attended and graduated from Stanford University with a degree in physics. After graduating from law school at the University of Michigan, he moved back to Kansas City and entered a general law practice. He often hunted with Nell on the family ranch and was spotting for her when she shot her last deer at age ninety-one.

After a full and rewarding life, Nell died in her home in Kansas City on September 8, 1991, at the age of 102. Her son, David, died in the summer of 1998.

## FOR MORE READING

The *Dictionary of Missouri Biography* (Columbia: University of Missouri Press, 1999) has an excellent profile of Nell Donnelly Reed written by Donald B. Oster. The same volume also includes entries for James A. Reed, John F. Lazia, and the Pendergast brothers.

*Kansas City Women of Independent Minds,* by Jane Fifield Flynn (Kansas City: Fifield Publishing, 1992), sketches the lives of many successful Kansas City women, including Nell Donnelly Reed, giving a good sense of the community and the context of their lives.

There is a biographical sketch of Nell Donnelly Reed by Yvonne V. Jones in *Show Me Missouri Women: Selected Biographies,* edited by Mary K. Dains (Kirksville, Mo.: Thomas Jefferson University Press, 1989).

Unpublished papers relating to Nell's business are in the James

A. Reed papers at the Western Historical Manuscript Collection at the University of Missouri–Kansas City.

*Enterprising Women,* by Carolyn Bird (New York: W. W. Norton, 1976), a Bicentennial Project of the Business and Professional Women's Foundation, discusses Nell Donnelly in "Fashion for Everyone II," in chapter 19.

# Afterword

Each of us, woman or man, is born to a historical time, and it is our challenge to make the best of our lives. For the earliest humans and for us today, that has always been true.

At the dawn of the twenty-first century, men and women alike benefit from the gains made before us. People today can choose their occupations based on what they like to do rather than accepting the roles once assigned to their sex. Some women choose careers in business. Some men enjoy staying home. Increasing numbers of us decide not to marry or, if married, not to have children. We explore many paths, find out what we do best, and live full lives.

That is not to say that men and women work the same way and bring the same strengths to their tasks. Indeed, men and women bring real differences to the jobs we take on. Scientists have learned that on average, women have remarkable endurance and that women's brains are good at keeping track of several things at once. This special characteristic helps women do three or four tasks at one time. At home, we might chat with a neighbor while reading a recipe and stirring the soup, still with an eye on the kids in the living room. At work, we accomplish multiple tasks as we negotiate over the telephone, jot notes from the conversation, and check a new e-mail message from an office assistant—all at the same time.

For the extraordinary women in this book, endurance and the ability to do more than one thing at a time meant survival and success when they faced hardship and adversity in their lives. When they were called to courage, they responded with thoughtful action. Although separated from us by decades of change, their lives are gifts to us as we persevere against the challenges of our own times.

# Index